PEACE
on
EARTH
HANDBOOK

PEACE on EARTH HANDBOOK

LOREN E. HALVORSON

AUGSBURG PUBLISHING HOUSE
Minneapolis, Minnesota

PEACE ON EARTH HANDBOOK

Copyright © 1976 Augsburg Publishing House

Library of Congress Catalog Card No. 75-22718

International Standard Book No. 0-8066-1516-8

Scripture quotations unless otherwise noted are from the Revised Standard Version of the Bible, copyright 1946, 1952, and 1971 by the Division of Christian Education of the National Council of Churches.

Manufactured in the United States of America

CONTENTS

06913

Suffering is the power of the powerless.
Violence is the powerlessness of the powerful.

Helmut Frenz

Preface

This volume is something between a book and a catalog. Perhaps it is best explained as a scouting report. That may be too military a term for a source book on peace building, but it seems to describe my own experiences over the past quarter century exploring the territory between institutions of the church (congregations, colleges, seminaries) and the frontiers of direct engagement in society of the people of God.

The work of a scout cannot be done if the scout is confined to the barracks. Nor can the scout's assignments be fulfilled if no reports are ever brought back to the main body of troops. The reports in the next pages come from some unknown territory, but I hope they are presented in a way that makes sense to the reader. Scouts may get some strange ideas while living in unexplored areas. Throughout these chapters you will encounter this scout's struggle to put his own beliefs and experiences into a meaningful framework. That framework includes refugee work in Germany in the late 1940s, parish ministry, seminary teaching, and an international assignment in the area of peace and justice.

The language of faith and social issues are interwoven in the fabric of this source book. The same is true of local and global perspectives. The patterns that emerge may seem confusing, and that is characteristic of the world in which we live. But I hope that two basic convictions stand out clearly: (1) the resources we need for peace building already exist, and (2) they are hidden in those closest to us. To link up those who share these beliefs is the purpose of this little volume.

Israel sent scouts into the Promised Land the first time the people in exodus reached the borders of Canaan. Most of the scouts were frightened by what they saw. The people believed their report and chose not to venture any further. That generation perished in the wilderness. But a few of the scouts heard and saw something quite different in the new land. Perhaps they were not believed because they were not as eloquent as the others. Or perhaps the people lacked the courage of faith.

Today newspaper headlines, TV documentaries and prophets of doom portray a dismal picture of the future toward which the human race seems headed. Even young people find little excitement contemplating the future. This source book on peace building may be a minority report and it may not be as eloquent as the mass media and the choruses of experts. But those who make it believe deeply in what they have seen and heard. Among those are Jørgen Lissner, LaVonne Althouse, and Charles Lutz who helped gather this report.

1

Peace Building: God's Gift and Everybody's Business

The "There-is-nothing-we-can-do" Myth

"This is Walter," said the person at the other end of the phone. I recognized the voice of Walter Tengelson from New York, director of one of the many projects connected with America's effort to put astronauts on the moon. I had met Walter some months before in his home on Long Island where he had patiently explained to me the complexities of systems engineering, the art of planning and managing a great variety of activities in such a way as to produce a desired result. "People don't realize," Walter had said at that time, "that the real breakthrough in the space program was not technological, such as the invention of some new hardware. The important breakthrough was figuring how to put all the pieces, people, manufacturers, government agencies, and especially very independent experts together to accomplish a common goal." Walter had a fancy name for this planning process. He called it "trans-systems analysis." I never had the courage to tell Walter that I didn't understand

11

most of what he was talking about, but I was intrigued with the ideas he stirred in my mind.

Suddenly, the conversation was interrupted by explosive noises on Walter's end of the phone—sounds of people shouting, dancing, and what seemed to be champagne bottles being uncorked. "Walter, what in the world is going on?" I asked.

"Aren't you watching your television set?" asked Walter.

"No," I answered, "I'm in my office at the seminary looking at shelves of books and student papers."

"Then you missed the news," explained Walter. "Just this minute the astronauts landed safely in the Pacific Ocean, completing the first successful manned exploration of the moon. The staff here has been watching the whole thing on TV monitors. They have worked for ten years on the project and are celebrating."

"Walter," I said, "You were directing that particular staff all these years. How come you are on the phone with a theologian at the very moment when your colleagues are throwing a party?"

"Well," replied Walter, "I'm not really excited anymore about putting people on the moon or Mars. What really interests me these days is the application in other fields of what we learned about getting very different kinds of people and organizations together. I would like to apply some of those discoveries to dealing with human problems here on earth. I think you people in the churches ought to apply these same approaches in order to mobilize the immense human resources you have to tackle the social problems that are tearing our society apart."

The last report I had from Walter some years later concerned his efforts to help the mayor of New York

City straighten out the mess caused by the garbage collectors' strike. But the unusual telephone call that day set me thinking about the human resources in the churches throughout the land. Maybe Walter said it or perhaps it welled up from some earlier experiences working with the laity of the church in Europe and America, but from somewhere came the thought, "Perhaps all the resources we need already exist and our problem is that we don't know where to look for them."

The impact of the 1960s on our society and institutions has led some people to ask, "What can we do?" But many more people seem to be asking, "Can we do anything at all?" The sense of powerlessness can easily paralyze the unleashing of just those efforts needed to bring about meaningful change and to achieve social justice, peace, and reconciliation.

This book is meant for such people, especially those who ask such questions within the framework of the Christian faith. It challenges the "there-is-nothing-we-can-do-about-it" way of thinking and suggests that the place to begin is to discover what God has already done and is presently doing in the world for peace, justice, and healing. We may discover that Walter's expectations were not misplaced. There are more possibilities than we have ever realized, if we are willing to explore the potential of the future.

An Unwilling Journey to Jerusalem

Since the time of the Exodus, the journey of God's people into the future has been a reluctant one. Helmut Gollwitzer, the well-known German theologian, describes his prisoner of war trip into Russian Siberia as an "unwilling journey." The disciples were not eager to accompany Jesus on his journey to Jerusalem. But despite this reluctance Jesus "set his face steadfastly toward Jerusalem" (Luke 9:51 KJV). The disciples had good reason to be afraid of that journey. The consequences of it were the arrest, torture, and death of Christ, the apparent tragic end to a brilliant ministry, the collapse of the dreams of many for a new age, and the bitter disappointment of Jesus' followers who had expected the overthrow of the repressive religious and political systems.

Suffering, apparent defeat, and destruction have often characterized the journeys of God's people into the future. We are, therefore, often afraid of the future. Today that fear is particularly strong and threatens to paralyze the desperately needed efforts of ordinary people to seek a world of peace. The future can be a new beginning but its uncertainties demand of us courage and trust to discover the potentials hidden by our fears.

The Problem/Possibilities of Grace

The future will elude our grasp if we key off problems only. There is little hope of unleashing the potential resources you and I have for peace building in a problem-centered approach. Human problems are eloquently reported, filmed, telecast, and illustrated in today's mass media. If we continue to emphasize only the enormous problems facing us, we could easily push this generation off the brink of despair.

Furthermore, an approach that sees only the problems and locates evil in others and not in ourselves avoids the heart of the matter. The comic-strip character Pogo put it simply, "We have met the enemy and he is us." Continued war between peoples and

14

nations to destroy the evil identified in the other is as disastrous a course as the early twentieth-century notion that good will and prosperity will solve our problems.

We need a strategy that takes fully into account human sin and the disruption of our relationship with God and with our fellow humans, as it takes seriously the possibilities for the human race, barely visible in our deepest yearnings, but clearly revealed in God's acts of grace toward us. We need an approach to the future which keys off from grace. Then, perhaps, we can face the hard facts of social, economic, and ecological crises and not panic, and face evil head on but see behind it possibilities for grace. Behind staggering problems lie even more surprising possibilities which faith unmasks behind the facade of the problem-ridden world.

The global community of the future must learn to live in unprecedented intimacy without war, to face honestly differences in belief and behavior without polarization, to become sensitized rather than thwarted by differences of religion, race, sex, age, political, and economic systems. The world that faces us contains the most intensive concentration of all the elements that in previous ages have caused conflict and war.

Can the problems of racism, economic justice, ecological abuse, and human rights violation be transformed from conflict to peace building? How can they become possibilities? The perspectives and experiences of different peoples in the world are necessary for the health of the world community. Rather than flattening out our differences or removing the uniqueness of each or producing a homogenized mass, we need to discover enrichment through diversity. The threats of conflict between black/white, rich/poor, male/female,

15

young/old, secular/religious, sick/healthy, North/South, and East/West are generating deep fears in people today, but they also contain the possibilities for healing. The very differences, for example, which the female experience provides pose a profound threat to a male-dominated society conditioned to resolve differences by combat. Yet this very "threat" is the most widely dispersed problem/possibility in our time for learning the things "that make for peace."

Is this vision of the problem/possibilities of the future so demanding that it leaves you paralyzed? What can you, an ordinary person, do? Between the prophets of doom on the one side and the utopian voices on the other we need a third alternative. We need the example of practical people stirred by a vision of peace but with their feet solidly in a particular community, working there on do-able alternatives. We need level-headed and cool global citizens willing to work with what is (which means with ordinary people like ourselves) in order to pioneer what might be. This book is for such people.

The "Terror" of the Possible

Deeply embedded in each of us are dreams of what might be. We resist the notion that the course of history is fixed, determined by the relentless momentum of economic or social forces. The biblical view of history asserts that neither the gods, historical fate, or established laws fix our future. The future belongs to God. And God has placed it in our hands as a gift. That is the terror of the future. What frightens us most is not the uncertainty of what will happen but the realization that we are responsible for what does happen. The future is in *our* hands, not somebody or something else's. That awesome discovery could tempt us to act as if we were God, or it could sober us to a deeper trust in God.

We need visions of the future to renew our weary spirits. Human dreams have been badly mauled today by the cynicism which has resulted from decades of conflict. Too few people think in terms of alternative futures. Of course dreams can become detours from present tasks, a kind of "future pietism," a raising of expectations which seem to be quickly dashed. But dreams can also produce practical actions. At the end of the 1960s some friends and I attempted to evoke ordinary citizens to respond to the racial crisis in America by inviting local action groups to share their positive efforts toward peace and justice through a new kind of national conference we called the "People's Fair." Scores of displays sharing the extraordinary things some ordinary people were doing were set up in a convention hall. It was a celebration of what already was possible.

The purpose of sharing these "acts of civil courage" was not only to raise hopes but also to provide practical examples, graspable and do-able alternatives for people who felt there was nothing that they could do about the future. The unleashing of the resources present within average persons requires the raising of their hopes through the eloquence of alternatives demonstrated by people like themselves.

What ordinary people can do, what many indeed have already done, is reported in the next pages. Part of that story is the history of experiments in citizen mobilization in Europe and North America during the past two decades. Part of that story is the movement toward more lay involvement in the church following World War II. That story is the subject of the next chap-

17

ter. The following chapters seek to document the on-going story of people power for peace and justice through parables illustrating peace-building activities from various parts of the world and in practical suggestions about how you can become involved.

2

Discover What Is

Public Scrimmages

In November 1966 residents of the Minneapolis-St. Paul area were invited to a month long community discussion of current social issues under the general theme "Care of the City." Television documentaries, radio talk shows, films, and several hundred resource persons made available to community organizations raised issues for public discussion. There had been violence in the Twin Cities that summer, and many people felt the need for an open and frank discussion of community issues. Augsburg College in Minneapolis received a federal grant to enlist the assistance of twelve other institutions of higher education in the area to spearhead the program. It was hoped the experiment would create a climate for informed and honest dialogue.

The public discussions in the Twin Cities in 1966 were inspired by a similar program in Germany called the "Church Week." In the 1930s sensitive leaders of the German churches were alarmed at how skillfully the Nazis were stilling the voice of conscience by gaining control of many of the vehicles of public discussion. Such forums as trade unions, professional societies, schools, community organizations, political parties, and even churches were being intimidated by Nazi propagandists. Free and open discussion of critical issues, such as the Jewish question, was becoming increasingly difficult. In order to counteract this, a bold program called the "Church Week" was inaugurated to bring to a particular city a team of articulate and well credentialed spokespeople in different areas to stimulate public discussion. The team of resource persons was led by the bishop. The week of community discussions began with an official reception in the city hall with the mayor and the city council. Then followed appearances of the team in the schools, professional societies, churches, civic organizations, and newspapers. For a while, at least, some controversial questions appeared on the public agenda. But the Nazis were not enthusiastic about public dialogues in those days and soon prevented the movement from continuing. The idea went underground for the duration of the World War II to be revived in the Church of Hanover by the dynamic new bishop, Hanns Lilje.

The idea of trying such an approach in the U.S.A. grew out of a lay school of theology in Brookings, South Dakota in 1963. At the end of a three-day series of lectures by imported theologians one of the lay participants remarked about the experience, "It was all quite interesting. But I still would like to know what it has to do with my work at the feedmill." That comment triggered a long discussion in the parsonage among participants and guest lecturers. In the midst of asking how the issues of faith could be meaningful for the feedmill, someone suggested that instead of gath-

20

ering people for chalk talks in church buildings, some form of scrimmage ought to be tried within the community itself. At this point the idea of an American version of the German "Church Week" was born.

In a very few months a local committee in Brookings organized what came to be known as the "Faith in Life Dialogue." Some 50 resource persons were enlisted from various parts of North America. Such areas as law, medicine, education, agriculture, theology, family life, and business were ably represented in the team which was led by one of the pioneers of the German Church Week, Bishop Hanns Lilje. During the five days of the Brookings event nearly every regular meeting in the community, in schools, in civic organizations, in business and professional groups, and even in home kaffeeklatsches had a Faith in Life topic and guest resource person. TV and radio programs, articles in the local papers, and films in the local theater spurred local discussion. The local movie house had packed audiences of paying customers watching *Judgment at Nuremberg, On the Beach,* and *Billy Budd.* After the showings the theater became a public forum as the audience discussed the film with a panel of resource persons on the stage. Several mass meetings, musical groups, and theatrical performances added artistic input to the stimulation of public discussion.

The following year a second Faith in Life Dialogue was attempted in Fargo-Moorhead and in 1965 again in Duluth-Superior where the event was called the Northern Lakes Dialogue, extending across Northern Minnesota and Wisconsin. The mass media became the major vehicle for bringing the program to many scattered communities throughout the region.

At this point in the experiment, however, some basic changes in the program were made before the

21

next attempt was made in the larger setting of Minneapolis-St. Paul. One week was seen to be too short a time to maximize citizen participation. More emphasis on using local resource people was urged. Lower overhead costs were also suggested by utilizing outside persons who might be brought into the community at the costs of local groups rather than by the planning committee. Also more small group discussion and action were urged. The most visible change, however, was in the name. The religious community did not serve well as the sponsor for a public forum. The schools seemed to be more acceptable common ground for that. Therefore, the planning committee in Minneapolis and St. Paul decided to turn to the institutions of higher education in their cities for help and to call the event "Town Meeting."

Town Meeting

In the early years of the United States, town meetings played an important role in involving all the citizens in the villages and towns of the New England colonies in the public discussion of local issues. The town meeting tradition has left its mark on American society in the cherished practices of free speech, citizen participation, and volunteerism. With the growth of larger cities the direct participation of all citizens became more difficult. Such efforts as the chautauqua meetings tried to revive the town meeting in the 19th and early 20th Century. With the advent of radio broadcasting the "Town Meeting of the Air" attempted to recover the earlier tradition, even though radio audiences were not direct participants. In 1959 Washington University in St. Louis and the local educational

22

TV station joined forces in the Metroplex Assembly in which several hundred small viewing groups meeting in homes, churches, and schools over a period of several months watched weekly documentary TV programs, discussed them, and phoned in their opinions.

The Town Meeting of the Twin Cities in 1966 drew on all of these previous experiences. Six months in advance of the November Town Meeting the churches, schools, civic organizations, and institutions of the area were invited to use their regularly scheduled November activities to discuss one of forty topics under the theme, "The Care of the City." A study booklet provided discussion materials and instructions on how to use the mass media and resource persons provided by the local planning committee. Twenty-seven theaters scheduled films relating to Town Meeting topics, and several hosted discussion periods in the theater after the film. All the local TV stations and many of the radio stations participated. Although intended as a one month effort, the Town Meeting continued through the next spring, primarily through programs of the educational station KTCA.

At the same time as the Town Meeting in the Twin Cities was attempting to generate public discussion on current social issues, other communities in North America were pursuing similar efforts. The Goals for Dallas program, also in November 1966, followed a similar format. In Harrisburg, Pennsylvania, the educational TV station developed a Town Meeting type program. In Canada a program called "Town Talk" was attempted in the Lakehead region. Eventually the Town Meeting was attempted in New York City in 1973. During these same years a nationwide "town meeting" was developed in Holland and still continues;

it is known as the Peace Week. Adaptations of the Dutch program have been attempted in Sweden *(U-veckan)* and Germany *(Friedenswochen)*.

In the restive 1960s town meetings, however, were still seen to be too "talk" orientated without sufficient action resulting. Furthermore the basic process was dependent on mass media and therefore was seen as too vertical, that is too "top-down." People were being informed and stimulated, but they were not really active participants, taking responsibilities into their own hands.

The limitations of this one-way mass media communications became clear in a 1968 meeting of national representatives of the mass media in America called by John Gardner, director of the National Urban Coalition, to discuss the implications of the Kerner Report for the communications industry. Representatives of the Twin Cities Town Meeting were there to explain their effort to generate citizen participation. The leaders of the national media were hard-pressed to show how their audiences participated in any significant way in their programming. The best example they could provide was a four-week documentary series on the race issue which resulted in an "avalanche" of letters. But when pressed as to how many letters from the reported 22,000,000 viewers of that series constituted an avalanche unprecedented in the network's history, the answer was "about 200." Obviously mass media alone does not provide much citizen participation.

Communi-action

In 1969 the decision was made to radically alter the Town Meeting approach. Instead of massive input from the media and reliance on outside "experts," the program was to be primarily in the hands of the partici-pants themselves. Efforts were made to shift from vertical communications (heavy reliance on TV and radio programs or prepared study materials from some central office) to lateral or horizontal communications in which people looked not up for answers and re-sources but around among friends and neighbors in their own local area. What resulted was a program called "Communi-action" (actually the misspelling of "communication").

During Lent, 1970, the Protestant, Catholic, and Jew-ish communities in the St. Paul-Minneapolis area were invited to organize small viable action groups, that is groups of people who had a common turf in which to act: family, neighborhood, congregation, industry, or professional groups. Some five hundred groups were organized; they met mostly in homes, but were not limited to members of the same denomination. During the seven-week period of Lent the small groups ex-plored the needs in their community in housing, edu-cation, welfare, and consumerism. They were not told by experts what the problems were but discovered for themselves through a simulation game called "Dignity," weekly field assignments, reality quizzes, and group interviews with local resource persons through a tele-phone speaker device in each home or meeting place.

The Communi-action program was an upside-down Town Meeting. There was still some use of mass media. The groups were invited to watch a documentary on TV especially prepared for the occasion. But after a few weeks the field assignments precipitated so much discussion that many groups no longer watched the TV documentary during their meeting. There was also a distinct movement from discussion to action. Through the telephone speaker device the groups also interviewed people who were attempting to do something about the problems under discussion. As a result many of the groups became involved in some direct action as they considered not only problems but also possibilities.

It was a time when people were asking, "What can we do?" Communi-action demonstrated that people can discover answers for themselves in their own communities or institutions and can undertake some meaningful action. An evaluation of the Town Meeting approach had already indicated that mass media by itself did not generate much activity or change basic attitudes. The initiation of some action and a change in attitudes seemed to occur more readily in small groups tackling an issue at the local level where they could do something about it. The shift away from the Town Meeting "vertical" communications to the "horizontal" people-to-people, "look around you in your own neighborhood and do what you are able" approach of Communi-action affirmed the hunch some of us had that God has already deployed the resources of the kingdom everywhere (often in the most surprising places) and seems to delight in hiding them in those closest to us!

Right in Your Backyard

I have recounted the story of recent community communications experiments in order to make the point that in the midst of crises, or perhaps because of crises, there are more resources for peace building around us than we recognize. Perhaps we have been so blinded by the problems that we cannot see the possibilities near at hand. We are very much like the disciples of Jesus who were told, "The kingdom is in your midst."

They didn't see it because they didn't believe it. And if we never look we never find.

This is the thrust of Christ's admonition, "Seek first the kingdom of God and all these things will be added unto you." I believe that the "seeking" and "looking" part of that familiar verse is understood too spiritually in terms of purity of purpose or high-minded aspirations so that the very practical implication of this truth is overlooked. Everything needed to realize the purposes of God in the world (the supplies for meeting the needs of our neighbors in whom God encounters us) is *very close at hand*.

That discovery led the organizers of the Dutch Peace Week to shift from the global to the local and led those of us experimenting with Town Meetings and People's Fairs in North America to start looking in our backyards (or micro-communities) to deal with the problems pressing on people from above (the macro-communities).

I can best describe the "look in your own backyard" idea through some personal experiences in looking for participants for a national Action Models Fair in the late fall of 1969. In connection with the Communi-action program and a seminary course on Church and Society the Nicollet Hotel in Minneapolis was reserved for three days to host a fair featuring peace building activities that people were doing to respond to the social issues in American society. I began looking for possible participants by checking with national organizations and offices: government bureaus in Washington, D.C., denominational offices, mass media networks, and the like. I was told what national groups were doing, but not about the ordinary people who were doing extraordinary things and for whom the fair was intended. Much to my amazement, the most

27

helpful leads resulted when I was referred to resources literally in my own backyard.

I remember a telephone call to a friend in the American Film Academy in Washington, D.C. who was working with volunteers from Hollywood such as Otto Preminger and Sidney Poitier to assist youth in urban ghettos to make films about their own life situation. I had seen such a film made by teenagers in Harlem which profoundly affected the audience. In response to my question my friend told me with great enthusiasm about a high school teacher who was making films with her class in English literature. Two members of the class were arrested for shoplifting, and the teacher soon became involved in the case. The result of consultations with the police, store owner, and the two students was the production by the two students of a film on shoplifting. The experience had a marked effect on all involved—a healing experience for the students, store owner, and police. When I inquired how I might get in touch with the teacher who had since left that community, my friend gave me an address over the phone of an apartment I could see from my seminary campus.

On another occasion I contacted a group in San Francisco which had been reported to have a computerized inventory of volunteers in the Bay Area. But they in turn referred me to Jim Siefkes, one of my own colleagues, whom I had not asked because I was not aware of what he was really doing. On Jim's desk I found an old recipe box filled with grass-roots action models from all parts of the country—exactly the things I had been looking for during the past weeks in New York, Chicago, Los Angeles, Washington, D.C., etc. Jim's desk in the national church offices where we both worked was just 50 feet from mine.

The most dramatic experience of being led to one's own backyard came during the Action Models Fair itself, when a friend from Germany, Reinhard Schmidt, came bursting into the hotel auditorium where the displays were set up and shouted at me, "Mensch, ich hab' es endlich entdeckt!" ("Oh boy, I have finally found it!") When I finally calmed Reinhard, he explained how he had been traveling in Japan, England, Scandinavia, and North America on a research grant to discover ways by which TV could become a two-way communications tool allowing the audience to participate actively in programming. In a federal office in Washington, D.C. he had been told about two young men who were experimenting with a process that could turn telecasting upside-down. During the Fair, Reinhard had discovered them in St. Paul operating a program with the weird name CADAVRS (Computer Assisted Dial Access Video Retrieval System).

Together with the local educational TV station they had put together a library of some 1000 five-to-ten minute film documentary clips covering a wide range of subjects to supplement instruction in the local schools. Teachers could order any items they wanted by push buttons on a little black box attached to their classroom video tape machine and have that item for class the next day. The customer had control over what was telecast. The next step the inventors were working on was to make the system globally available through communication satellites.

I do not believe these experiences are merely accidental. In subsequent years I have experienced again and again, especially in small groups, that there are more resources at hand in the persons present or through information they have than anyone had imagined.

It makes a great deal of difference if you begin with what *is* rather than with what *ought* to be. Too many speeches, sermons, and books tell people what they ought to do. "Ought" language does not seem to inspire much response. An honest look around at what *is* can be discouraging but it also can be filled with surprises. More than likely we are apt to discover that somebody is already doing what we think ought to be done. There is no need to re-invent the wheel, but that is what often happens when we begin with "ought" rather than "is."

The Action Models Fair began with "isness." The displays from that initial fair were put into a truck and toured 36 states. The truck became a roving retrieval vehicle picking up new displays from the colleges, church conferences, shopping centers, and auditoriums where the traveling fair was set up. Some extraordinary things being done here and there by ordinary people quite unknown to even their neighbors were discovered and added to the growing number of displays.

The idea of People's Fairs began to spread. In Iowa, for example, the North East Iowa's Human Resource Center, helped pioneer a new kind of country fair. Instead of sharing the latest farm machinery or grandma's pickles, people came together to share what was going on in the county to meet human needs. Some years later a Human Resource center was established at Clear Lake, Iowa.

In planning the 1975 convention of the Iowa District of the American Lutheran Church the decision was made to begin with what is. The convention site became a fair grounds, as various groups and individuals put up displays of what they were already doing in church and community. The formal legislative and decision-making activities of the district were set in the

30

midst of a visual environment of "isnesses." Most conventions produce what ought to be done, but not much usually results. The Iowa convention chose to celebrate what already was happening and to find ways to enable efforts which already existed. In Iowa a bold step was taken to develop a new type of meeting in which the diverse agendas of the participants gave direction to the overall activities of the district.

Meeting As Shalom

Meeting people is an important part of peace building. The greeting "shalom" or "peace" is a message shared by friends and strangers alike since biblical times. Meetings in the modern world, however, are seldom peace-making encounters. The different and often opposing agendas and expectations make of many gatherings a painful and tense affair.

Is it possible to create meetings which match the different expectations of people? The complexity of the task, not to speak of the current mood of disenchantment with meetings in general, does not make the work of a convention committee an easy one.

Consultations, meetings, assemblies, workshops, seminars, committee sessions, make up a large part of the organizational life of society. The expenditure of time, money, and energy required by these efforts and the paucity of results have driven many to search for alternatives. Attending a meeting too often detours or blocks getting our own agenda accomplished. Therefore, it is not surprising that there is a certain "meeting fatigue"—if not outright resistance—to meetings abroad in the land.

The problem is by no means new. Philip Melanchthon is reported to be the author of a Latin couplet which reads, "In conferences our lives transpire, that in them we finally expire!" (Maybe he wrote that after the 15th draft of the Augsburg Confession.)

The complete rejection of meetings of all kinds would, of course, be a tragedy—especially for Christians. At the very heart of the life of faith are the gatherings for worship, renewal, mutual upbuilding, celebration, edification, reflection, and action. The communion of saints means encounter, fellowship, corporate life—in short "meeting." So the question is not "to meet or not to meet?" but "what happens or what fails to happen when we meet?" An analysis, therefore, of the forms and functions of meetings may be helpful to discover the relationship between form and substance, method and meaning, program and purpose.

For the church, however, the type of meeting is not just a question of methodology but one of theology. The church meets to celebrate, ponder, and communicate the work of God in the world. Is it too much to say that church meetings properly belong to the Third Article of the Creed? That they are potential openings for the Holy Spirit? If so, then there must also be a sense of mystery, surprise, the unexpected, a sense of a larger task, a greater agenda when we meet and consciously seek the guidance of the Spirit.

But how does one combine careful planning, specific agendas, down-to-earth tasks, the daily operational needs of organizations and agencies with the mystical, spontaneous, charismatic aspects of God's surprising agenda? That agenda regularly interferes with our own. No organization is likely to plan its own demise, yet God calls people to lose their life for God's sake. No group votes itself easily into crisis, conflict, and controversy. "Don't rock the boat," is the usual watchword of institutions. Yet crises, tragedies, and defeat

32

are often the very vehicles "in, with, and under" God calls people to service and renewal. Furthermore, if the church meets under the Word of God, that Word is first of all addressed as a word of judgment to the church herself, as Bonhoeffer argued in a 1939 article "Protestantism without Reformation." If that word is to be heard at a meeting, confrontation, conflict and radical questions are to be expected. Meetings of Christians, therefore, are fraught with danger—as well, of course, as with grace.

The drive for self-preservation is so fundamental a force that efforts have to be made continuously to keep meetings open. And for the church with her "serve God—serve neighbor" orientation, this means open to both the Spirit, and to others, and to the Spirit through others. In the Puritan Revolution Cromwell instituted debates in his army to determine the will of God, since his followers rejected the guidance of church hierarchy. But in order to guard against a simple majority vote to determine what the Spirit was saying to the people, a minority report was also permitted—just in case the Spirit chose to speak through the minority.

Perhaps the question of "form, style, process" in meetings could be put in terms of whose agenda should prevail. All would agree that it should be God's agenda, but through which group is God addressing us today? Through those with global or local perspective? Through formal or informal systems? Through "sacred" or "secular" means? Professional or lay? Theory or practice? The powerful or the powerless? Through those who say "yes" and then do not do the Father's will or those who say "no" but then do the will of the Father? The church of the Reformation with its original history of radical critique of church councils, its emphasis on the priesthood of all believers, and its concern to translate liturgy and Scripture into the language of the people has good reasons to strive consciously for open meetings and to suspect approaches that are predetermined and closed.

Increasing Participation

Pentecost was an "international" gathering of people from many lands and languages which achieved communication between diverse peoples, inspired them, and propelled a missionary church into the world. Intriguing as it is, however, to suggest Pentecost as a model for meetings, our course as sinner/saint creatures lies somewhere between a thoroughly planned and ordered procedure *and* a spontaneous, charismatic event.

These two aspects can be combined if we seek full participation of all: young and old, rich and poor, elite and non-elite, conference "pros" and beginners, clergy and lay, the extraordinary and the ordinary, people seeking renewal inside and those seeking it outside the structures. The movement toward increased participation is of importance to the church not because of some western "democratic procedures" model but because of the concern to be open to the various gifts of the Spirit expressed in the many members of the body of Christ.

Recent church history has been moving in the direction of increased participation. Post World War II theology stressed the doctrine of the church in terms of the whole people of God. Great emphasis has been placed in recent years, therefore, on the role of the laity. And this emphasis has broadened and deepened from increasing awareness to the role of the people of God within church structures (lay training, stewardship, small group work, evangelism) to increasing awareness of the role of the people of God in society (social action, justice, community development). While we are still critical of our institutions and procedures falling short of the ideal of full participation of all, a great deal of progress has been made in that direction. For example, when professors begin teaching each fall, they probably have to negotiate with the students regarding the course assignments rather than dogmatically announcing them.

Perhaps because of more exposure to problems of social injustice, racism, and the misuse of power, we have become more aware of the issue of participation in terms of the poor and oppressed. "How are the poor and powerless to be heard when the church meets?" raises a far deeper and more gospel-related question than the concern for democratic procedure. In the famous letter of the Mekane Yesu Church this concern is stated in several ways but most poignantly in the plea for the church to be concerned with "unimportant" people. The well-known Lutheran church historian, Martin Marty, commented recently on the church's neglect of her "unimportant" members: "The whole character of our writing about the church has been misconceived, misdesigned. . . . We wrote our history too much from the viewpoint of formal theologians or ecclesiastical politicians . . . not from that of the bulk of the people of the church. I have a hunch most historians will be reworking their programs in the years ahead."

Enabling the "Least" of These

Dr. Lambourne *(Church, Community and Healing)* and Dr. Siirala *(Voice of Illness)* speak of a "caring

35

community" which recognizes in the anguish of the sick and weak the symptoms of the sickness of the whole community. The weakest are the ones who suffer most quickly and acutely the injustices of society. The weakest link in a chain under pressure is the first to break. The natural reaction of an organism is to reject the diseased part. So called "developed" Western societies tend to remove or "sanitate out" the ill who have become dependent (aged, mentally ill, poor, "undesirables") rather than viewing them as early-warning signals of the attitudes and priorities of the strong and "healthy" members. The test of the health of a community is the way it treats the weak in its midst. Hence they use the terms "caring" or "healing" community rather than an "efficient" or "developed" community.

What kind of meeting or convention would result if the planning were to focus on the weakest? If the test of success is not efficiency but "healing?" What would happen if the principal clients were to be seen as the delegates who are there for the first time, the representatives from the most precarious situations, the smallest, the most timid, the least secure, the most easily overlooked or forgotten, those with the least power, those whose voice would not be heard unless amplified by a "caring" assembly?

The Morphology of Meeting

In considering the form or style of meeting a simple diagram can provide a spectrum of options between the two extremes of a totally planned and ordered procedure and a completely spontaneous "Pentecost."

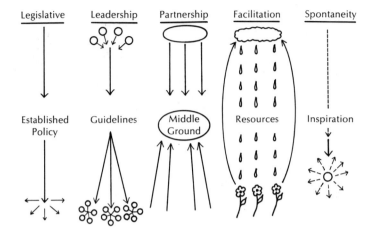

Legislative	Leadership	Partnership	Facilitation	Spontaneity
Established Policy	Guidelines	Middle Ground	Resources	Inspiration

Legislative

In this pattern the program or policy determined from above (or from the outside) requires conformity at the local level. In some respect some mission boards have operated in this way, enforcing strategies determined from the outside. Such a procedure need not necessarily be destructive, providing the control group has an unusual degree of wisdom, omniscience, and grace.

Leadership

The second type attempts to take account of diverse agendas at the local level by creating a more broadly representative leadership group and seeking to re-create at a lower level counter-part machinery. However, the basic structure remains top-down: basic policy and priority decisions are made outside or above the local situation. This approach has been taken in some council of churches systems which have

37

tried to reproduce the same structure at lower levels. The Swedish *U-Veckan* used a similar approach starting with a nation ecumenical council providing leadership to 200 local councils.

Partnership

In this model there is an attempt to provide a balance between initiatives from above and below (from outside and within). A common ground or neutral territory is required as a "missing" arena between the two levels. At the 1973 *Kirchentag* something like this occurred at the "Shalom Forum" which provided a platform for various groups to interact. Although some fringe groups distrusted the ecclesiastical turf of a *Kirchentag* and did not participate and too little cooperation between local action groups and church leaders resulted, still it was quite effective and was tried on a more thorough scale in the 1975 *Kirchentag*.

Facilitation

In situations where there are strong local leadership and resources the facilitation model seems to work best. Stimulation, encouragement, and support are provided to enable the achievement of initiatives already under way at the local level. This could be described as a communications model and seems to be the emerging function today for national and international bodies. The Dutch Peace Week illustrates this approach in which the national planning group sees its role as a catalyst by sharing ideas and resources in response to local action groups.

Spontaneity

In this scheme local groups are so independent and self-reliant, they need little if any supra machinery.

This is perhaps an idealistic view of the church, although it has been attempted by some sects. Even the early Luther believed for a time that with the Bible and the Catechism in the vernacular the local congregation would need no clergy—not to speak of bishop and church council! The Youth Congress stimulated by the religious community of Taize has attempted this scheme with almost no central planning—only the inspiration of an idea spread by word of mouth. The very effort could generate more responsibility because of the large dosage of freedom—or it could result in chaos. Perhaps the brothers at Taize dare risk this because their lives are deeply rooted and disciplined in the Spirit.

Toward a Combined Approach

When you consider the diverse expectations of the participants, it is clear that no single approach will work. The challenge of an assembly today is to design a combined approach, a mixed system, which allows for a number of processes to happen: festivals, legislative activities, information sharing, fellowship, education, workshops, worship, net work building, etc. It also seems advisable to find a good balance between careful planning and flexibility. In brief, is it possible to do a number of things at once and do them well all within one cohesive event?

An article published in the early 1950s on the history of the *Kirchentag* and German Evangelical Academies (lay training centers) was entitled, "Between Cloister and Committee." It raised the same question about the possibility of providing a place where both prayer and debate could be brought together. This can be done and has been done. The German Evangelical

Academies attempted to provide a platform for discussion between groups which often were antagonistic to each other. That effort required a combination of careful planning, openness, tact, trust, and risk. In recent years more attention has been given to greater diversity in approach: small group work, closer cooperation with local parish, field work, and communication.

The *Kirchentag,* of course, represents an effort on a very large scale to combine a number of activities in one event. In recent years the *Kirchentag* has consciously tried to increase the participation "from beneath" so that smaller and more peripheral groups might share with traditional church organizations in the planning and execution of the event. The trend has been clearly in the direction of greater participation and flexibility. The same trend has been obvious in our attempts in North America to adapt the *Kirchentag* to a different church and social context. The first efforts were more massive, total community campaign affairs called "Faith in Life Dialogues" and later "Town Meetings." But after a number of years of attempting to stimulate the interaction of faith and daily life within the immediate local context it became clear that the scale had to be personal and local, yet the national and global aspects of the issues could not be forgotten.

Recent Experiments

By 1968, aided by a research grant to evaluate the results of such church and community efforts, it was clear that it was necessary to link within the overall process action and resources at many levels: personal, local community, regional, national, and global. Subsequently some practical applications were attempted. One was designing a convention for the United Church of Canada. Another was a national conference on "Building Communications for a Future Environment" for the National Urban Coalition in which a planned plenary program, workshops, a "market fair" to display and exchange ideas, and informal encounters all took place simultaneously. Another effort was a massive ecology effort in the Pacific Northwest of the U.S.A. combining mass media, government agencies, and community organizations.

Still another opportunity came in designing a "People's Fair" process in response to the urgent plea after the riots of 1967 and 1968 in American cities, "What can we do?" The fair toured 26 states and was part of a number of church conventions. About the same time the same ideas were used to design a nation-wide effort in Canada called "Man and Resources." On the basis of these experiences there were also such "mixed systems" approaches in international settings. One was a meeting in Driebergen, Holland, in 1970 and the other the meeting of directors of lay training centers in Crete. In this latter case there was a particularly good response from the Africans who had already developed a "market fair" approach to conferences.

This history of the search for a combined approach of involvement of people in a common process could be documented in other parts of the world and in other types of organizations. There exists already a good deal of experience in this field. Not all the experiments have succeeded well. Some have been poorly conceived and planned. The challenge would be to combine solid planning with an open process in which there is a maximum participation of all. To do that it would be helpful to identify what are the different components in the total process and to prepare each one carefully.

Components for Helping People Meet
The Plenary

This provides the arena for the legislative activities or other gatherings of the entire group for business, worship, or lectures. A variation on the form might be a setting of participants around tables to make it possible to go quickly from plenary to small groups, especially if it is desirable to have delegation groups discuss issues before voting.

The Workshop

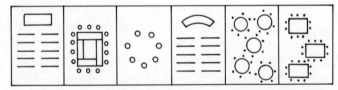

Facilities in which smaller groups can meet to work, discuss, plan, organize, edit, etc. during or between plenary sessions. This component would be especially useful for various departments and committees to work on their specific agendas during the meeting and take advantage of the resources gathered there.

The Market Place

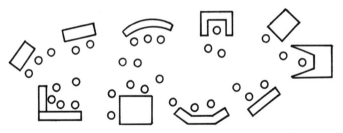

A promenade or hall of displays attended by persons directly engaged in the project or activity. This is a very flexible component to which can be added displays at any moment. It has remarkable potential for retrieval of existing programs at any level.

The Meeting Place

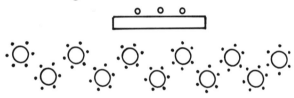

A "coffee house" or lounge provides a place for informal meetings which sometimes prove to be the most valuable dimensions of a conference.

The Information Booth

A central information booth easily accessible to all is essential to bring people into contact with each other, inform participants of activities, link groups or persons together quickly, and counsel the bewildered. With loudspeakers and projection equipment, announcements and requests can be instantly brought to all participants.

The Theater

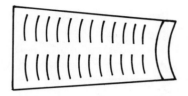

In this room or rooms films, plays, special briefings, and lectures can be held on a scheduled basis, repeating presentations of special interest at different times.

The Forum

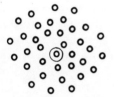

Places for "feedback" where everyone has an opportunity to express his concerns. These could take the form of "Hyde Park Corners," the most open and accessible to public forums.

The Resource Center

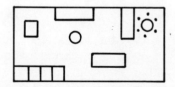

The central office for supplies, printing, typing, and getting any resources needed by individuals or groups during the assembly.

After planning each of these components well, giving some thought of how to keep the scale and place manageable for planners and participants, informing the participants so they know what to expect, and doing all we can so that we come prepared to work, share, discover, and plan together, *then* we can pray for Pentecost.

The Potential of the Lay Movement

The type of people meeting described above and the citizen mobilization experiments like Peace Weeks, Town Meetings, and People's Fairs are all direct fruits of the lay movement in the 1950s. I believe it is important to recognize this because the concern for peace and justice is an important aspect of the growing awareness of what it means to be God's people in the world. I would like, therefore, to sketch briefly the history of the lay movement in recent years and suggest where it may be going in the future.

The close of World War II was one of those moments in history when people consciously looked for a new beginning. The victims of the war, burdened with grief and shock, hoped for something better. The victors were optimistic that improved societies would result with the "right" people in control. But there were some who were more realistic and knew that only the future would demonstrate whether a new beginning had been made or not.

There were predictions within church circles in those days that an era of the laity had begun. Theologians gave fresh attention to the understanding of the church as the people of God. Pastors and church officials concerned themselves with equipping the laity for their ministry in the world through programs of lay education, centers for renewal, and scores of books on the subject. After a quarter century of efforts to inaugurate an era of the laity, the question can be raised whether or not these expectations have been achieved.

What is happening today "beyond the sanctuary" with the "scattered ministry" in "dialogue with the world" (to quote a few of the popular cliches of this era)? Has the concept of the priesthood of all believers enunciated by most Christian churches, been realized?

An obvious answer to such questions would be an immediate, "Just look at all the new activities." And the list is impressive: lay training centers (like the German Evangelical Academies), huge rallies of up to hundreds of thousands of lay people *(Kirchentag),* lay officers in church institutions, small groups of every possible description, theological training for the laity, mountains of literature on the subject, reports, consultations, commissions, committees—certainly enough documentation to keep historians in the future employed for some time.

The issue of the role of the laity has been caught up in recent years with the debate over the church's role in society. Almost every denomination and congregation has experienced some polarization over the interpretation of how the church should respond to social issues. The question of the "dispersed people of God in the world" has become even more urgent and serious. Perhaps we are only now entering the age of the laity, as the issues of the world press upon the church.

A strange thing happened to lay education on its way to the world. It became more and more sensitized to the issues of peace, justice, and the healing of the community. Dialogue about the faith is giving way to direct action; the classroom is being replaced by field experiences; theologians who have been guiding lay reflection are discovering their own reflection being guided by lay experience. Outside experts are giving way to the involvement of local people. Instead of extraordinary people attempting ordinary things, ordinary people are being enabled to do extraordinary things.

Perhaps in the next quarter century, as the work of lay training becomes more "secular" and as church members become more engaged in the community, the lay movement will also become more religious. Clergy and laity need to probe together the mystery of what generates the hope and sustains the power that unleashes Christian ministry in the world. Perhaps the concept of "peace building" will take on new meaning as a growing sense of our responsibility for the future is combined with the Christian affirmation that the future is God's gift to the whole people of God. If both the altar and the street become the setting of lay training, historians in years to come may then find ample evidence to claim that this was indeed the era of the laity.

3

Look Around, Down and Close By

In Unexpected Places

"Look around rather than up" sounds irreverent. But I do not think it is offensive to God, who has already dispersed the resources of the kingdom. Those resources have, in fact, been deployed in the most surprising places. And that is why we have such a hard time finding them. We are likely to be looking in the wrong places.

Most people do look *up* to get things done. Our culture has conditioned us to look up to the experts, the authorities, those above us to solve problems. Because so many people expect solutions from "up there," authorities are being over-burdened with mounting expectations. Often those in positions of leadership are expected to accomplish tasks beyond their competency and power. There is also a powerlessness amongst the powerful. That powerlessness is the inability to do what can only be done by people themselves in their own particular situation right where they are.

49

There are many legitimate expectations that should be made of the people above us, but first, we should spend more effort looking around. Then we may discover it is not always necessary to look up. The other side of this equation is that those on top—the experts, professionals, leaders—need to "look down" for the resources they need.

The phrase, "look down" sounds derogatory, and often this is the case. Too many "authorities" suffer from an elitist blindness to the resources to be found among the unsophisticated, lay, non-professional, ordinary, powerless people. If more persons in position of leadership looked down first, the expectations on them would not be so paralyzing. God has indeed deployed the resources of the kingdom in surprising places.

The following stories or parables on peace building are intended to illustrate this last point. The final part of this chapter contains some reflections on the implications of looking around, down, and nearby, especially among the powerless.

When Did We See You?

When the Son of Man shall come in glory with all the angel hosts, all the people of the world will assemble before him to be judged.

And he will say to those who have been sent to stand at his right hand: "Come, you who have been chosen for blessing because your lives have been blessings to me. For when I was banned and exiled from my homeland for doing justice, you let me visit you, listened to my sorrow, and protested until my own people again received me and listened to me. When I was beaten and sweating in prison, you rescued me with the

50

weight and persistence of your protests. When I and my family were starving, you pressured those who employed me to pay me a living wage. Though pressed on every side wtih concerns of your own family, community, and congregation, you did not ignore my cries but lent me your strength and support."

And to those who have been sent to his left side, he will say, "Depart from me, you who are hardened and indifferent, and trapped in the concerns of your own family, congregation, and community. For when I was exiled, you did not receive me and help me. When I was in prison, you spoke not a single word on my behalf. When I and my family were starving, you watched the telecasts, said, 'That's dreadful,' and turned off the set and the memory of our suffering. Go, therefore, where all is cold indifference and suffer the isolation and loneliness and pain of those without the support of a community of love and concern that reaches out forever."

Then a loud clamor arose from both sides of the judgment chair. "When did we see you exiled, or imprisoned, or hungry with your hungry family and protest and pressure for your restoration and relief?" asked voices from the right.

From the left will come wails and cries of protest: "When did we see you exiled or imprisoned or hungry with your hungry family and ignore your misery?"

Then, raising his hand for silence, to be heard over the rising clamor, he will say: "Whatever you have done on behalf of the brother or sister most distant from you, the one for whom society and conscience tell you you have least responsibility, you have done to me."

adapted from Matthew 25
by Lavonne Althouse

Theology of the Hoe

"You mean a theology of the *whole*," I replied in my best up-to-date Geneva language, a bit surprised that my friend had not kept up with the latest theological developments in Europe despite his isolation in a seminary in Brazil.

"No, I mean a theology of the *hoe*," answered Dick with emphasis. Dick Wangen is a teacher in practical theology in the Lutheran Seminary in Sao Leopaldo, Brazil. "Are you acquainted with the writings of Jose Comblin?", he asked.

Now it was my turn to question who was up to date in theology. "No," I replied, wondering how I could regain the initiative as the enabler who had come to Brazil to help the pastors in their seminar on "Church and Community."

Wangen then went on to explain a very simple and human process whereby theological students live and work with the poor to learn the meanings of their words and expressions. After six months they write up a diary in the new language they have learned, describing the people's beliefs about God and life. Their theology as young seminarians was being shaped in the context of the poor. Out of this exercise, Dick explained, new liturgies were prepared in the language of the people.

Latin America: Community Building from Beneath

Exciting evidence of growth and vitality at the local level can be found in Latin America where the need for support communities is great. There, in situations where political and economic restrictions limit the

52

field of direct participation in issues of social justice, remarkable initiatives in small groups are emerging. This may be the unseen revolution in Latin America, not nearly as dramatic as the much heralded "theology of liberation." Perhaps, like the "theology of the hoe," in the long run the direct work of ordinary people toward social justice and humanization is more significant.

Often the work must be carried out quietly if not secretly. One example is a center for rebuilding community among laborers in a South American country where the labor movement has been nearly destroyed. A small group of Catholic priests are devoting their energies to the quiet but crucial work of helping people develop the courage and possibilities to determine their own future in a society which had all but destroyed their hope.

A similar point was made by a group of 57 families —all political refugees—living in a camp and seeking as a group to emigrate out of Latin America. Somehow under the stress of a common fate, driven to rely on their own resources, and facing situations under which communities usually break down, they found a strength in each other that is usually absent in affluent and so-called free societies.

The Fraternity of the Sick

Among the many examples of basic community groups the one I find most inspiring and remarkable is the movement called "the Fraternity of the Sick." Originally begun by a Catholic priest, this movement starts with the least likely candidates for building community. Often the sick are the ones who pathologically remove themselves from normal community life. In this program the sick are located, visited, and encouraged to articulate their feelings. They are helped by patient listening to face their condition and then are invited to a festival in a community building or church. A worship service, a feast, and a community celebration made up of the halt, the lame, and the blind turns out to be a happy affair. The event itself requires the mobilization of the healthy to transport the sick, beds and all, which creates a scene of the faithful assembling that could come right out of the Gospels.

Community development workers in Latin America report that celebration is an important first step in building community. But gatherings of the populace are often difficult because they are politically suspect. But when the church gathers the sick for worship and fellowship, no one can charge the church with a "political" act, for she is fulfilling her historic and biblical ministry. Yet such behavior has profound social implications. All social classes are involved in the Fraternity of the Sick for disease and physical handicaps know no social distinctions. The rich and the poor meet on the commonness of their human frailty. And since the sick are among the most vulnerable to unjust political and economic structures, they provide a kind of social barometer for the state of the community's health: an immediate and clear revelation of the real quality of life.

Efforts to build or rebuild human communities among the sick and estranged may be so local and frail as to miss the attention of outsiders. Yet they provide a potential which if multiplied—and they are replicable because they depend solely on the resources of the people themselves—could have vast significance toward peace and social justice. The "Fraternity of the

Sick" is also a parable of the churches' transforming role in situations of oppression through the destitute. In weakness and suffering the greatest impact of the gospel is made.

Support from Others

Easter morning, and the streets of the South American city were deserted. My friend and I sat in a cafe visiting with a young university professor who had lost his teaching position the previous year when the government had closed the university. Because of his activities in the cause of justice and peace and his close friendship with political leaders who were in prison, his future was a precarious one. He was also an active member of the student Christian movement in his country. "How is it," we asked, "that you continue to remain here when half of your colleagues on the faculty of the university have fled the country?"

"I suppose," he answered, "it's because of the support community of which I am a member. Come along and I will show you."

We were taken to a new apartment building where 33 families lived. Most of them were friends through the student Christian movement. Some had been members of experimental communities which had not succeeded. But now they had formed their own cooperative and built their own apartment. On the first floor was a school for their children and common meeting rooms. "We have most of our meals in common," he explained, "but we have also learned how to balance that with the privacy of family life." He then explained the regular meetings of the group including worship experiences.

"This is my support," he continued. "We would each

be very vulnerable in the present political situation of our country. But here we have a solidarity which gives us strength and hope." He went on to inform us that just a few days previously one member of the group had been arrested. But there was no panic. Not a single family had left the country, although large numbers of their friends had. Where two and three gathered to form a community new strength and power was found. We left that night depressed by what was happening to a nation under a police state, but strangely encouraged by a small community which was finding new life by sharing it.

Vegetables Can Be Flowers

Minnie had two sons, LeRoy and David. David, the younger son was a mongoloid. "He will remain a vegetable," Minnie had been told. But she and her husband refused to accept this fate and devoted their lives to helping David become a self-reliant human being. LeRoy became a famous geneticist exploring the mysteries of genes to discover how defective births like his brother's could be prevented. But as a devout Christian LeRoy also pursued the ethical and theological questions of genetic defects. "Who will play God and decide whether Davids have a right to exist?" asked LeRoy as he toured the country, wrote articles and books, and made TV appearances.

I first met David through a film made by LeRoy at the state university where he taught. The first part of the film described the advances in genetic research and suggested that the day was not far off when genetic controls might prevent a David from being born. Then the film showed the life and activities of David who at 30 years of age had become one of the

56

most loved and loving persons in the community—
thoughtful, happy, gentle, and amazingly self-reliant.
"Does David have a right to exist?" asked LeRoy at the
close of the film. "On what grounds—moral, religious,
legal, social—should he be refused life?"

The scene in the film I shall always remember
showed David at the dinner table praying the Lord's
Prayer. The camera moved in on his lips as he struggled
to form the familiar words, "Our Father. . . ." His halt-
ing and haunting petition in language barely under-
standable was one of the most beautiful prayers I have
ever heard. The memory of it leaped into my consciousness the night I received a telegram from LeRoy's
wife, Elizabeth, with the shocking news of LeRoy's
death in a private airplane accident.

Some years later I met David and Minnie in the
church where they are active members. Minnie, in her
late eighties, is still remarkably active. She and her
husband cannot move into a retirement home because
David is under 65. David is kept busy in the congregation serving on committees and helping others at
every opportunity. At the request of the shut-ins David
has been commissioned by the congregation to bring
Holy Communion to them. His warmth, gentle humor,
and devoutness have made a profound impact on that
community.

Minnie continues to ask "why" concerning her two
sons. But she also marvels at the strange way the weaker of the two has become such a powerful resource
for peace in the lives of troubled people.

The Women at the Well

Sometimes the only power people have is their
poverty. That was the case in the story of a group of

women in an urban slum in Colombia, South America. In their hillside slum on the edge of the city there was no water supply. They had to carry their water from a contaminated stream which was more like an open drainage ditch. One day they were visited by a representative of the International Fellowship of Reconciliation who suggested that they should organize themselves into a group and bring their problem before the city authorities.

The first meeting between the mayor and the women was most cordial. They were warmly received, their petitions heard, and promises were made to install a water system within three months. The women were elated. They had not expected that it would be so easy. But after three months nothing had happened. So they visited the mayor again.

The second visit was not so pleasant. Some harsh words were spoken. Excuses were given by the authorities. But finally an agreement was made that work on a water pipe into the slum would begin within three months. However, after the three months had passed there was still no sign of activity on the part of the authorities.

The women met to decide what to do next. They realized that they had to take some action or nothing would be done. They had no money, no experience in community organization, no advocates among those in power. All they had was their poverty. So they decided to use that.

In the theater and restaurant district of the city where the rich sought their evening pleasures a beautiful new water fountain had been constructed. It was the pride of the same authorities who were reluctant to lay a simple water pipe into the slum. The fountain sprayed a beautiful pattern of water into the air, but the wind often blew the falling water on the pavement. Around the fountain were pools of water.

One night when the theaters and restaurants were filled and the city square where the fountain was located was crowded with people, ten women from the slum came with their babies and began to bathe them in the pools of water in the street. The sight shocked the well-dressed theatergoers. Some of the women dressed in long evening gowns went up to the slum mothers and said, "You stupid people. Don't you know your children will get diseases from the dirty street water?"

"Yes, we know," replied the poor women, "but this water is no different than the water we have to use daily for cooking and bathing in our slum."

The policeman on duty came over to the mothers and ordered them away. "This is a public place," they protested. "We have made inquiries and were told that there is no city ordinance against washing our children here."

Perplexed by such a response from the poor, the policeman went off to the station to report to his superiors. Soon he returned with other officers and took the women away. No sooner had they left the square than another group of ten women from the slum turned up with their children and began to repeat the same action. They too were escorted away. But then another group of ten arrived to take their place. By that time a large crowd had gathered. Some of the wealthy women, including a few wives of city officials, had by then gotten the story directly from the slum mothers. Shocked by what they had heard and seen, they joined the women from the slum and protested the action of the authorities.

Not long thereafter a contingent of women appeared at the mayor's office. This time there were women from the upper classes among them. And this time the mayor acted. Fresh water now flows into a South American slum because some poor people discovered an unexpected power in their poverty.

The Jury That Refused to Quit

"But I have never made a public speech before in my life," protested Joyce as she faced hundreds of delegates at a national church convention. Joyce was a member of a jury which had recently completed one of the longest trials in American history. For eight and one-half months she heard testimony concerning the Wounded Knee case. Ninety-eight days of this time was devoted to government witnesses bringing charges against the leaders of the American Indian Movement who had participated in the Wounded Knee affair. Only five Indian witnesses had been brought forward by the defense, but what they said had made a profound impact on the jury.

The members of the jury had been carefully screened by the government to make certain they were not involved in any movements known to be sympathetic to Indian groups or had ever made a public act such as writing to a senator or representative. They were authentic "silent majority" types. But now 12 of the 16 jury and alternates had chosen to speak and to perform their first public act. For the first time in American jurisprudence a jury formed itself into an advocacy group on behalf of the Indians and sent the following letter to the Attorney General of the United States. The letter read:

Dear Mr. Saxbe:

For more than eight months, beginning in January of this year, we have served as jurors at the Wounded Knee Trial of Dennis Banks and Russell Means. From the outset we approached the evidence in the case as impartial observers who had been selected by the government prosecutors and the defense lawyers. Possibly more than any other group of citizens we have had the opportunity to hear the facts and to judge them.

As you know, we voted unanimously to acquit both defendants of the charge of conspiracy and we were continuing on with our work when one of our number suffered a stroke. The Justice Department refused to permit a jury of the remaining eleven to reach a verdict; Judge Nichol granted a motion to dismiss all the charges against both of the defendants.

We think it is important for you to know that while all of the jurors undertook their obligations very seriously while we were a jury, some of us believe that our obligations continue. It is for that reason that we have written this letter.

We, the undersigned, wish you to know that we could not have voted to convict either of the two defendants on any of the charges and that we would not have voted to convict because each of us concluded that there was not enough evidence to do so in spite of the fact that the government presented evidence for 98 days and the defendants' response was comprised of but five witnesses. In our view a government that cannot, in an eight-month trial, present enough evidence against the two leaders of the Wounded Knee siege to secure a conviction on any count should for moral and ethical reasons, drop the criminal charges against all of the other Indian people and their supporters. Since the two leaders were guilty of no crime, we believe that others should not be prosecuted for following them.

It is in the spirit of reconciliation and redemption that we urge you to respect this suggestion and to join with us and other Americans in an effort to bind up the wounds that have been caused by this, our longest, and perhaps our least honorable, war.

Joyce finally summoned the courage to stand before the convention and explain why she had taken this step. She shared the consequences of her decision amongst friends and colleagues at her place of work. Some were supportive, others hostile. It had been a costly act. Questions were raised from the floor of the convention. The audience had been obviously impresseed by what Joyce had said and by the speeches of the Indians and one of the defense lawyers which had preceded her. Finally a farmer from North Dakota, a delegate to the convention, approached a floor microphone. His response was not what most had expected according to the reports of citizen reactions to Wounded Knee from the Dakotas.

"The day my wife and I left home for this convention," he began, "the government brought in earth-moving equipment to take over my farm for a water diversion project." He went on to explain how he had been unjustly treated by the authorities. How he had

attempted to get the government to place other farmers on the review boards hearing his case but to no
avail. Finally he said, "I know now what it means to
have my land taken away. I too, like the American Indian, am part of an oppressed minority."

Joyce's first public speech was not delivered with
polish, but it had an eloquence that gave courage to
others.

A Global Network on the Farm

"You can only make so much for your grandchil-
dren," says Verona Devney, a remarkable Catholic lay
woman who has organized Operation H.O.P.E. (Helping Other People Everywhere) from her farm house
near Northfield, Minnesota. She was talking about
many older women who love to knit and sew. As one
who had been active for years in mission work, she had
become increasingly concerned about the poor. She
had discovered that even a few concerned people can
do something. Together with friends she had managed to secure a boat for a missionary in Oceania. The
real story of H.O.P.E., however, began with the 800
yards of surplus textile goods.

Mrs. Devney went to the library to get addresses of
textile manufacturers whom she could approach for
surplus material for her local mission group to use
for making items for the poor. A half-dozen letters to
textile firms resulted in more than 800 yards of material delivered to her door step in one week! "I went
to mass that Sunday and all I could think of was all that
stuff. And then God led me to the other churches in
town." Operation H.O.P.E. began with an inter-church
group of women discovering a unity in doing that they
had never known before.

"I'm not so much for helping the poor, as shaking up the rich," says Verona Devney. "We scrounge for what is left over in America. We just take what people are not using. We match the rich and the poor. It's a crime that some can have so much and others so little." The matching up is done by ditto machine, telephone, and volunteer workers. "We never have much money in our treasury. I think that is the way God wants people to operate—not by enormous grants which take away the challenge. I just love to pick and scrounge."

Letters come to operation H.O.P.E. from all over the world from people in need. The ditto machine reproduces the letters, and a network of concerned people receive the requests. An appeal for help from 20 destitute families in Appalacia resulted in responses sufficient for 700 families. Mrs. Devney supplies the link between those in need and those who have. The rich and poor, the powerful and the powerless are her clients. Similar groups have sprung up elsewhere, but an informal voluntary network keeps them in touch. A warehouse of people and materials has been discovered by Operation H.O.P.E. A few ordinary people are discovering the extraordinary peace-building things they can do with what they already have.

Power of the Powerless

The preceding stories are about people who appeared to have little power yet did some remarkable things. Most remarkable of all is the way they used the power they had. I want to take up the theme of the power of lots of small people, but first I think it would be instructive to see how Christ understood power and how he used it. When we examine the way Christ used power, we see immediately the contrast to the way power is used in human institutions. Christ gave special attention in his ministry to the powerless. His compassion was drawn again and again to the weakest persons in the community. Christ relates to his people not as a hierarchical authority but as the servant of all.

Human institutions, however, tend to operate with power from the top and resist any effort to redistribute power. Institutions are not created for giving away power but rather for preserving it. Losing one's life for the sake of others is hardly the management principle of any institution, including religious ones.

Power itself is not evil, although people are constantly corrupted by too much of it. The true vocation of power, like love, is to seek the welfare of the other. The biblical case for human rights is not based on the political concept of democracy, but on the goal of God's love to help the powerless and to protect them through just laws which curb the ruthless use of power. In a sense the church has a social/political responsibility to live literally "at the disposal" of the weak and poor and to call those with secular power to exercise it on behalf of the powerless. Peace-building is what caring people do when they respond to the powerless.

But, you may well ask, how do you produce caring people? Caring people are converted people with a completely new set of priorities. Church leaders who operate from an opinion poll approach ("find out where the majority is going and then jump out ahead") are discovering that many rank-and-file church members are not prepared to make costly sacrifices for social justice. That requires a depth of commitment that most of us have not made and which our church membership by and large has rarely demanded. We are

65

now reaping the fruits of evangelism campaigns which were concerned too exclusively with personal salvation and stewardship drives which, despite the rhetoric, too often meant simply institutional growth.

The Gospel of Mark records the occasion when the disciples brought a possessed child to Jesus whom they could not help (Mark 9:14-29). When they asked, "Why?" they received the terse reply, "This kind cannot be driven out by anything but prayer."

I do not believe that Jesus' answer meant that the disciples should give up, disengage themselves, or withdraw to the sanctuary. They were not being chided for being activists. Jesus was reminding them of the basic fact that what was needed was a power far beyond their own resources, wisdom, and zeal. The incident from Mark might well apply to the apparent powerlessness of the church before unyielding social problems today. The deeper crisis is the lack of spiritual power.

Perhaps you like many have some questions about the social activism of the church. Sometimes such fears are well-founded. But we should remind ourselves that the biblical emphasis on social justice is very clear, and we should also note that the deeper Christians are drawn into human crises the more central and urgent the questions of faith become.

In recent years there have been concerted efforts in countries like Holland, Germany, Canada, Sweden, and Denmark to raise the understanding of people regarding conditions in the poorer nations of the world. These efforts have involved massive public educational programs through schools, churches, and mass media to inform citizens about "third world" countries. But, strange as it seems, the most effective conscience raising appears to have occurred when local issues have been the point of departure rather than global ones. Recent Peace Weeks in Holland and Germany have, in fact, chosen as their theme, "Peace begins at home." Although this sounds like a return to isolationism, it actually represents an important discovery that people's local agendas are the best starting points toward greater sensitivity toward the oppressed in other parts of the world.

The question of the use of power for social justice finds its deepest and most sensitive focus today not far away in poorer nations, but right at home in the relationships between men and women. Women are the most universally dispersed and most ancient of powerless groups. They are even called the "weaker sex." The question of the role of women is probably the most explosive of all human rights issues because it is the most universal. No society or institution is excluded. Here the culprit is not the North, South, East, West, black or white, rich or poor, but every social system and class. Here the problem is not a remote one of what others "out there" have done, but the painful question of how half of the human race has treated its closest neighbor.

The misuse of power right at home is an issue that has been pushed so deeply into the subconsciousness of both men and women and constitutes such an explosive question that changes in this area will require a solid framework of forgiveness and grace. This is why it is so important to see change and conflict within the context of peace building. The conversion of which the gospel speaks is not a radical change unto death, but unto life. It involves speaking the truth, but speaking it in love. Evangelism involves a thorough and honest appraisal not only of personal attitudes but of social behavior and social institutions as well.

Preaching for repentance, therefore, does mix social issues, politics, human rights, and economics with religion because it deals with the whole gospel, the whole person, and the whole society.

The exposure of social injustice is a painful but necessary first step in the process of liberation and healing. The perceptions of the powerless are an essential factor in this process. In exposing the misuse of power, the weak find that they do possess a kind of power which the powerful do not have. Whether such exposure will ultimately be healing depends on the ability of all parties involved to handle truth, fear, and power sharing. The final result can be healing if truth can be spoken in love. That is the real power of the powerless.

4

The Power
of Lots of Small People

If Two and Two and Fifty
Make a Million

Dr. Manas Buthelezi was placed under the ban by
the South African government. This articulate African
theologian was forbidden to speak, to meet with more
than one other person, and to have his writings or
words mentioned publically. Banning is like a living
death and is designed by the apartheid government of
South Africa to still the voices like Dr. Buthelezi which
speak out against the injustices of that country. Dr.
Buthelezi worked on the staff of the Christian Institute,
which despite opposition continues to work for understanding and reconciliation between all peoples
in South Africa.

In the spring of 1974 the ban was suddenly lifted.

"How did that happen, Manas?", I asked one day
shortly thereafter.

"It was the power of lots of small people," he replied. "There were protests from the usual quarters

69

when I was banned—the United Nations, the World Council of Churches, the Lutheran World Federation, governments in Europe and North America. But I believe the real difference was the flood of protests from small groups in churches all over the world. Letters came to me and to the embassy officers of the South African government in many countries from Sunday school classes, confirmation students, Bible study groups, and many, many individuals. I don't think the South African authorities had expected such an epidemic. In this case it wasn't the big voices but the little ones which made the difference."

This chapter explores the power of people movements and especially the power of the church as the "human delivery system" with the greatest potential.

The most critical energy shortage is the lack of concerned and informed people using the energy they presently have to meet the human needs in the world. The energy is already there. It needs to be unleashed through small and do-able acts of civil courage rapidly multiplying throughout the world. There is an old freedom song which goes, "If two and two and fifty make a million, the day is coming soon, the day is coming soon."

The Alternative Peace Prize

"The award which you entrust to me . . . will serve to forward a new war—a war without violence—for the humanization of the world." With these words Dom Helder Camara, Archbishop of Olinda and Recife (Brazil), concluded his speech upon receiving the People's Peace Prize in Oslo, Norway. The event was the climax of a remarkable grass roots reaction against the decision of the Nobel Peace Prize Committee to pass over once again the name of Helder Camara, a courageous spokesman for the poor who had moved out of the archbishop's palace in Recife to live with the destitute. The Nobel Peace Prize Committee had instead selected the foreign ministers of the U.S.A. and North Vietnam. This decision proved to be very unpopular with many people in Norway and other European countries. But it proved to be the springboard of a remarkable people's action.

The suggestion was made that funds be raised for an alternative peace prize from the people in Norway and elsewhere. The idea sparked immediate interest throughout the country. People in farming and fishing villages joined with urban labor organizations and radical students in supporting the cause. Many of these were the same people who a year earlier had formed an unusual coalition of conservatives and radicals to keep Norway out of the European Common Market because of their distrust of the accumulation of economic and political power that it represented.

Village and town councils were contacted as the local initiators for the fund raising. The deeds and actions of the Archbishop from Northeast Brazil became household knowledge throughout the country. Mass media and leaders of government, church, and labor joined in the cause. Similar efforts sprang up elsewhere in Scandinavia, Germany, Holland, and France. As a result, in a relatively short time enough money was raised to grant a peace prize to Helder Camara that was three times the amount of the famed Nobel Peace Prize. But more important, millions of people began to think of peace in terms of social justice rather than the mere cessation of armed conflict.

The People's Peace Prize was awarded in the same historic room in Oslo where the Nobel Peace Prize

ceremony takes place. Introducing Dom Helder Camara
was the director of the People's Peace Prize Campaign,
Gunnar Stalsett, an official of the church of Norway.
In his remarks he said:

We have learned about the potentialities in
uniting forces across boundaries of different
political convictions and faiths. The action
originated in hundreds of heads and hearts
spontaneously. It sprang out of political indignation and dissappointment but also of deep
engagement with the non-violence strategy of
Dom Helder Camara. It was carried by a hu-
manistic vision. Its source of energy was above
all that person who has consecrated his life to
promoting peace and justice.

The action itself raised indignation—maybe
because it focused its searchlight also on our
own and our friends' participation in suppres-
sion and exploitation. It raised enthusiasm because it enabled common people to speak up.

The campaign has been an educational process for the whole people. It has focused on the
great war, the war between those who have and
those who have not. This is indeed the great
world war. It has raged for generations, it has
taken more lives than any other war. It is the
silent war, the weapon of which is hunger. The
loser dies of hunger, the winner of abundance.
Also in 1974 about 35 million people will die
of hunger.

The campaign brought this most important
peace issue in our time, the relation between
the rich and the poor world, into the most hidden corners of our country. It has brought

a new element into the attitude of our country. It has brought a new element into the attitude of many over against the third world: Our traditional charity must be supplemented by far-seeing political endeavours for a just distribution of the resources of the world. Charity is no excuse for one's own individual or collective injustice. The process of conscientization has only started. It shall be tested in our foreign policy, our development aid programs and our trade policy.

The People's Peace Prize has become an instrument for peace. It has become so both by making the donors conscious about and pledged to an ongoing struggle against oppression and exploitation, be it in the South or North, East or West. The People's Peace Prize has become an instrument of peace also by enabling the receiver of this prize to continue his work for the construction of peace. It has become an instrument for peace by uniting people of many countries in a common task. It originated in Norway, but had soon international response.

The money awarded Helder Camara is being used for programs of economic self-help in poverty-stricken northeast Brazil. Hundreds of European parliamentarians have again submitted Camara's name for the Nobel Peace Prize. But whether he wins that coveted award or not, the people have clearly stated their choice.

People's Movements

Power concentrated in huge political organizations or in explosive weapons has fascinated moderns. Vast amounts of energies are consumed in the struggle to control the centers of power. Oppression is defined in terms of the use or misuse of power concentrated in the hands of a few at the expense of the many. But there is another aspect of power which is easily overlooked. That is the cumulative effect of what in isolation are insignificant centers of power. The combining of many separate centers of energy which in isolation have little impact occurs in "movements." The secret power of movements is replicability. Movements occur when centers of energy rapidly multiply, reproducing themselves until a whole society is affected.

Strategies for change might be divided into two groups: 1. those which seek change through the concentration of power at a few points through the impressive massing of money or institutional power; 2. those which seek change through dispersed, reproducing cells. The latter was the genius of the early church and other movements where the powerless people who had little else than faith and individual resources operating in limited spheres took responsibility in their own hands. Changes occurred quietly and unseen so that the actors themselves often despaired that anything was happening.

There is a growing evidence that something like a people's movement for peace and justice is stirring in different parts of the world: consumer groups, citizen action groups, spontaneous and planned grass-root responses, silent and not-so-silent majorities finding ways to express themselves. In countries where voluntary association and more open forms of public expression are possible, this takes the form of direct action. Lots of small people using what little power they have are having an accumulative effect on their societies. And where such freedom does not exist,

74

small groups are forming as support communities for individuals unable to cope in isolation with oppressive situations. An oppressive society creates a condition which often drives people together.

"Where two or three are gathered," is an apt expression today for many seeking an alternative to concentrated power. This new outburst of energy at the personal and local level might be called the New Dispersion of Israel.

One of the puzzling things of movements is that they seem to occur spontaneously. They function best when not centrally managed. Their power is sustained through individuals linked with other concerned people. A movement happens when tasks are scaled down to the level where ordinary people can become directly involved.

Too many challenges are made on such a large scale that direct participation is beyond the immediate reach of most people. The genius of a movement is precisely the breaking down of issues into particular, do-able, human-size tasks which enable participation and therefore, unleash the small bits of energies otherwise paralyzed by a feeling of powerlessness in the face of gigantic problems. The mobilization of ordinary citizens requires a vision big enough to enliven human spirits but immediate enough for participative action. "Think big, but keep it simple." "Do it yourself together." These are the mottos of the micro-macro dimensions of citizen action for peace and justice.

Case Study: Program to Combat Racism

One program launched at the global level which seems to have enabled direct participation of small groups is the controversial Program to Combat Racism of the World Council of Churches. Most church activities at the international level provide for the participation of national executives and a few others. But the Program to Combat Racism seems to have generated direct involvement of many church people, as well as, strangely enough, many groups who consider themselves outside or on the fringe of the church.

The difference may be that this was one of the few programs at the international level which attempted to move away from words, resolutions, and study documents to direct action. This is perhaps the cause of the controversy over this program. "Words could be more easily ignored than deeds," states a World Council of Churches document. A Small Beginning commenting on the reaction of the distribution of Program to Combat Racism (PCR) grants at Arnoldshain in 1970. Words have been the church's main form of response to injustice, but when they disembodied from deeds they make little impact. "This program has brought the debate of Christian responsibility in the contemporary world down from the ivory tower and thrown it open to a much wider constituency."

The move from words to action may be uncovering a whole new constituency for the church. Marginal Christians and marginal action groups have responded to the Program to Combat Racism. The church in this program may be catching up with many "drop-aheads" who because of their earlier concern for peace and social justice have moved far ahead of the institutional church. "The cooperation of the PCR with informal groups without any ecclesiological status points to another question about the character of the World Council of Churches. Should it remain a council of established churches, or has the practice of its life

76

already changed the character of the Council so it is open to cooperation with every group which belongs to the body of Christ?"

The Program to Combat Racism may be a modern illustration of Christ's parable about the two sons. The first son publicly said, "Yes." He followed the course of a "word" response. The second son who publicly said, "No," responded eventually with deeds. The stated belief of the first son remained rhetoric without result and therefore was not to be accepted. But neither was the stated belief of the other son. For despite the fact that he initially said, "No," he eventually did act. The point of Christ's parable is that it was not the stated beliefs of the sons that were the final proof of what they truly believed, but their responses in action or non-action. Jewish believers in Old Testament times, grasped the necessary unity of word and deed quite well and were extremely reluctant, therefore, to utter the name of God. There is a demand that the utterance of the word makes on the one who speaks it.

Another lesson from the PCR program is the double context of words and deeds today. There is immediate context and a global one. "Few World Council of Churches programs have ever received so much support from the so-called grass roots—even non-church, secular groups. . . . The local program is global. A universal approach to the problem of racism and a common effort to combat it will be possible only if each church takes seriously the situation in which it finds itself. The universal struggle will find expression in local involvement, and the one will compliment the other."

An excellent illustration of the above points is the story of two students in Denmark who won a special award in that country for their effective work under the Program to Combat Racism. Their story also illustrates what a very few people can do to effect even huge global conglomerates. The story is told in detail because it provides an instructive case study of several aspects of global justice and peace generally unknown to the public.

David Versus Goliath:
An Anti-Apartheid Campaign

The South Africa issue hit the headlines in the Danish press on January 24, 1974. A 40-minute program on the only channel of the Danish television had focused on the situation of non-white workers in South Africa. The program reported initially on the uproar in Great Britain following the articles on "starvation wages" in British-owned enterprises in South Africa published by the newspaper *The Guardian* in March 1973. But then the major part of the TV program presented a long interview with two black workers from two different factories in South Africa. Through an interpreter, they told about minimum wages far below the so-called "poverty datum line", about defunct work committees, and about threats of dismissal by their bosses of any worker joining the large-scale strike in the region.

The public reaction in Denmark to this TV program was extraordinarily strong. Because the two workers interviewed were not talking about ordinary South African factories, but about factories owned by the Danish East Asiatic Company (EAC) and run by Danish managers. And the EAC is not just an ordinary Danish company. It is the largest company in all of the Nordic Countries; it ranks, in fact, among the 500 largest enterprises in the world and has an annual turnover of more than two billion dollars.

The EAC has branches or subsidiaries in more than 30 countries on all five continents. And close to 40 top managers in EAC positions around the globe function at the same time as honorary consuls for Denmark. The EAC relations with the present Liberal Minority Government of Denmark are also the very best.

The EAC—known by every Danish school child as Ø.K.—is in other words the pride of a small nation. For this very reason, the TV program caused a minor earthquake in Denmark. The company immediately responded by calling one of its leading managers in South Africa home to Copenhagen. The following week the EAC took an unprecedented step: it invited the mass media to the first press conference in the 77-year history of the company.

One of the reasons for the embarrassment of the EAC was the categorical way in which the company had repudiated accusations ten months earlier. In March 1973, shortly after the start of the campaign of *The Guardian,* the Danish newspaper *Politiken* published a series of articles by a Danish journalist who had recently returned from a visit to South Africa. He accused the EAC of paying "starvation wages" to its black workers in South Africa and of violating the Rhodesia sanctions. He quoted named EAC officials in South Africa to substantiate his allegations and gave detailed figures on salary levels and working conditions. These revelations preceded the EAC annual stockholders meeting by two weeks, on which occasion the chairperson of the EAC board of directors denied that anything reprehensible or illegal was taking place. But he did not provide any concrete evidence,

"We trust that people will take our word for it," he said.

At this stage, the Danish Program to Combat Racism entered the scene for the first time. In the newspaper *Kristeligt Dagblad (Christian Daily)* it posed three specific questions on the conditions of the non-white employees in South Africa to the EAC. The response was curt: the EAC saw no reason for supplementing the information already given.

The Effect of Careful Study

On March 4, the Danish Program to Combat Racism finished two extensive reports, one of them a detailed 11-page account of the omissions and misleading elements in the wage information provided by the EAC (for example, inclusion of overtime pay in calculations of average wages). The other was a listing of the various indications that the EAC does in fact violate the United Nations sanctions against Rhodesia. Both reports were sent to the Foreign Affairs Committee and to the press, and they convinced many of the newspapers that the EAC had not told the truth at its press conference. The chairperson and other members of the Foreign Affairs Committee complimented the PCR for its sober and substantiated reports, and efforts by one member of the Committee to raise doubts about the reliability of the PCR were clearly rejected by the other members.

The Rhodesia report caused the greatest stir; this was a clear case where not only moral standards but also legal provisions were said to have been violated. The report was studied by the Foreign Affairs Committee and forwarded to the Ministry of Justice, which concluded that "legal proceedings cannot be ruled out" and hence referred the case to the Public Prosecutor for investigation. The PCR accusations against the EAC were twofold: (a) the EAC branch office in Salisbury had engaged in import and export activities as late as 1972, more than five years after the coming into force of the boycott legislation in Denmark; (b) the boycott legislation is phrased in such a way as to make it virtually impossible for any firm to operate a branch office inside Rhodesia without breaking the law, for example, by transfer of funds to Rhodesia from abroad or by payment of taxes to the illegal Ian Smith regime.

All the mass media—including both the powerful one-channel television and many of the small-circulation local newspapers around the country which rarely cover foreign affairs—gave wide publicity to the matter, and the EAC felt compelled to issue a statement saying that it was not aware of having violated the law, but that it would "of course" close down its branch office in Salisbury if it was found to have violated Danish legislation. On the following day the EAC issued another statement listing 112 Western companies with branch offices in Salisbury; the EAC and the other companies were "hibernating" in Rhodesia, surviving purely on domestic business while waiting for "normal times," it was said. The hitherto unapproachable and incommunicative business giant was beginning to respond and speak.

Two weeks later the Danish PCR hit the headlines again. On March 20 the report on Danish business interests in South Africa (the Danish version of this document) was made public; it was sent to the Parliament, to the mass media, and to all the companies listed in the report. The television gave it very good coverage and included among other things a discussion between the chairperson of the Federation of Danish Industries

(Industriraadet) and the leader of the Danish PCR, Leif Vestergaard. The former admitted that the South Africa problem had not been given adequate attention by the Danish business community; he consequently announced that his Federation would launch its own investigation into Danish commercial relations with South Africa.

The investment report was also sent to the EAC with an accompanying letter in which the PCR expressed its surprise and disappointment that the company had not even replied to previous invitations to dialogue about the South Africa issue. The letter went on to inform the company that the PCR had gotten hold of hitherto undisclosed information on wage conditions and other EAC business transactions in South Africa. "We continue to hope that your company will voluntarily make this information public. In case this hope remains unfulfilled, we will have to consider seriously, whether we can justify withholding this information from the Foreign Affairs Committee of the Parliament."

The EAC response was prompt. The tone of the letter from the deputy director was curt; he maintained that the PCR reports to the public included "a series of incorrect and misleading allegations and distortions of statements," and that it would be impossible to respond to it by mail. But the letter ended, surprisingly, with the following words, "If you want, however, to have your material corrected, you are welcome to pay us a visit." The PCR accepted the invitation, and it was agreed to hold a joint EAC/PCR meeting on April 3. But prior to that came the culmination of the duel between David and Goliath: the annual EAC stockholders meeting on March 27, which turned into a major confrontation between the EAC Board of Directors and spokespersons of the Danish PCR.

82

The Pyrrhic Victory of the EAC

The PCR strategy for the stockholders meeting was carefully planned months ahead. A coalition of individuals and representatives of various anti-apartheid organizations had been formed already in early January. No less than four South Africa proposals from four seemingly unrelated stockholders had been handed in to the EAC for inclusion into the agenda prior to the deadline on March 1. The release of the investment report was deliberately timed to occur exactly one week before the stockholders meeting. And the day before "the battle" the leader of the PCR portrayed the PCR and its objectives in the prominent regular feature article of the leading conservative newspaper *Bedlingske Tidende*. This paper had been openly defensive of the EAC during the previous months and is read by many of the EAC stockholders. The article was a showpiece of moderation and reasonableness; no one could suspect the PCR of being a "leftist cover organization" or a group of hot-headed or misinformed activists.

This image of respectability and reasonableness was scrupulously safeguarded also during the stockholders meeting itself. The PCR spokespersons were chosen accordingly: a theology professor, a middle-aged marine engineer, a retired banker, and a middle-aged YWCA general secretary. In addition, the group of 22 PCR-related stockholders included one bishop and several pastors. Some of the students had to see the hairdresser before being accepted as participants! The meeting took place in one of Copenhagen's most distinguished concert halls, the Odd Fellows Mansion. More than 1200 persons attended, several hundred of them young EAC employees in their early and mid-twenties. Within an hour the usual business had been taken care of; only the last and unprecedented point on the agenda remained: "stockholder proposal concerning the activities of the Company in South Africa."

Four proposals were introduced one by one, and a lengthy discussion ensued. The board of directors reacted extremely defensively and flatly denied that its policies in South Africa were in need of correction or improvement. The atmosphere in the assembly hall was tense and initially unmistakably hostile to the PCR "trouble-makers." But gradually the general mood changed, and many of the stockholders—including quite a number of the young EAC employees—began to applaud some of the PCR arguments, either out of sympathy with them or out of uneasiness with the defensiveness of the board of directors.

After two hours of discussion, the board chairman made a final speech emphasizing the achievements of the company and its continuing sincere concern for the welfare of the non-white employees in South Africa. Then he abruptly brought the debate to an end by making the following motion: "The annual meeting endorses the line taken by the company in its activities in South Africa." The chairperson of the meeting immediately put it to the vote, ordered the ushers to collect the ballots, switched off the microphone and deliberately ignored several loud requests for point-of-order interventions from PCR representatives.

Except for a few pro-business newspapers, the entire Danish press strongly criticized the clumsy and arrogant conduct of the EAC leadership. Editorial comments reflected clearly that the EAC had won a Pyrrhic victory: "The heavy-handed behavior (of the EAC) has—presumably contrary to intentions—strengthened the critics of the company" (Politiken).

The financial daily *Borsen* commented that the EAC board chairperson had "taken the company two steps backwards after having taken it half a step forward," a policy which the paper labeled "reactionism."

With one or two exceptions, all those who had criticized and opposed the Program to Combat Racism (PCR) on theological grounds during its first two years of operation remained conspicuously silent all through the spring campaign. The *Kristeligt Dagblad,* which had initially been against the PCR, was now all in favor and gave excellent publicity to the campaign.

Denmark is but a small link in the chain tying the Western market economies to apartheid and South Africa. Seen in isolation, the Danish events clearly do not make much difference; but as part of world-wide efforts by concerned people to improve the lot of the non-white population in South Africa and to undermine the marriage of convenience between Western business and the regime in Pretoria, the Danish PCR action takes on some significance. In addition, the small size of the Danish nation (five million inhabitants) and the special structure of the Danish mass media (one TV channel, only three radio programs, and a limited number of nationwide newspapers) make for a "social laboratory" situation from which certain lessons can be learned. Finally, some encouragement can hopefully be derived by other groups around the world engaging in similar action from the recognition that a business empire is often no more than an image with feet of clay.

Laity and Citizen Action

Citizen action or volunteerism has been well developed in countries like the United States and Holland

and is growing in other European countries. We may be witnessing the birth of a new form of mission as church members become more informed and involved in local and global issues. Citizen action as the Christian's local view of mission calls attention to what might be called the "ecology of mission." Ecology of mission is a concept which stresses the utilization of the wealth of human resources surrounding the local parish as it faces the social and political tasks of its community. While some church bodies still attempt to operate in the hierarchical style of Christendom or in the adaption of business management styles, the future clearly demands participatory systems which recognize the potential of the church in penetrating society through the leaven of its members.

The potential of the church as the people of God dispersed into every arena of human activity—education, politics, and professions, community organizations— so loudly proclaimed in the 1950s deserves renewed attention. "Where have all the lay people gone?" one wonders in observing institutional church behavior. The time has come to recognize that the "movement" aspect of the church as the people of God hardly filters through ecclesiastical structures when they limit Christian witness to church institutional activities and ignore or forget—and thereby belittle—the laity's presence and potential in society.

Programs of citizen mobilization exhibit much more the characteristics of movements than institutions. A movement is sustained by indigenous efforts. Voluntarism will continue to happen not because of initiatives from above but from people themselves.

The genius of a movement is in the mobilization of the resources within local communities themselves, building on the commitments of the people there, and, through direct but informal ways, linking these efforts with similar ones elsewhere.

Let me use a simple illustration. Ideas thrive, multiply, and enter other bodies through cross-pollinization. Movements need "bumble bees" to pollinate other organisms ripe for fertilization. Perhaps the church as a movement grew originally in this apparent haphazard way rather than through carefully engineered plans. The best "bumble bees" for citizen mobilization are not officially appointed officers as much as ordinary people doing acts of peace building here and there in the world. Therefore, greater effort should be made in the future for contact between ordinary but involved people in international organizations and meetings.

There is something bracing, realistic, and challenging in the idea that "unless you do it yourself it doesn't get done." A self-sustaining, self-renewing process seems the best way to facilitate an international network of peace builders. When people get linked up lots of things can happen.

"The idea arose in the hearts and minds of hundreds of people at the same time." These words by Gunnar Stalsett, coordinator of the Alternative Peace Prize action in Norway, suggests that movements of direct participation are not solely matters of careful planning. They are also a mystery. Movements have to do with the human spirit and cannot be so easily managed. The involvement of the Christian community in social and political affairs by definition brings together the elements of mystery and planning, of faith and reason. The motivation of people's hearts and careful planning based on factual knowledge are both involved.

Earlier we raised the question some people have about the church getting involved in social issues. I think we must stress the point that if the church is to retain her integrity and be faithful to her mission in the area of social and political responsibility, then the dimension of mystery must be given high priority. The pace is being set for the church by the activity of God, by the work of the Holy Spirit in the world. But since this work takes place in human history, fidelity to what is actually going on in the world through factual study must also receive high priority.

Where Do We Begin?

The people of God are at different points in relation to Christian concern for justice, peace, and human rights. From these different points diverse views emerge that produce distinct groups in the church. There seem to be four main groups. These four groups are not to be pitted against one another, but rather to be seen as stages in the full sweep of Christian concern for peace and justice. We need to recognize the different contributions of each group and the different approaches needed to assist each one through its particular stage of development. Each needs to be affirmed but also helped toward an eventual understanding of the positions represented by the other three groups. This approach recognizes not only that there are different positions at any given time, but that there also is a process in development which results from new perspectives and experiences over a period of time.

Critical Evangelicals

The first group might be defined as critical evangelicals who are aware of the claims of the gospel for social justice, especially as these claims are interpreted in terms of the individual Christian. This group is concerned to keep the concerns for social justice deeply rooted in the gospel and closely tied with the mission of the church. They believe that society can only be transformed as new pastors are created by the gospel. This group has an essential contribution to make to the church's role in society by its insistence on a biblically rooted approach. Its individualistic approach can, however, easily detour the church from a maturing understanding of the tasks for social justice in society. This group needs to be encouraged to take further steps along its course of social concern, which for many means participation in activities of social ministry and direct Christian action. In other words, this group grasps the essential relationship between worship and public service.

Hopeful Activists

The second group represents those who have already moved into active social and political issues and are perhaps at the early stages of expressing their concerns in church-related welfare and social action programs or in acts of charity. They might generally be called hopeful activists. This group has the potential of moving from a social welfare level of involvement into more direct social and political action. They represent a transition stage from charity to justice. Often such persons are channeled into community activities through such programs as peace weeks and action fairs.

An impressive number of persons presently engaging themselves in activities for peace and social justice come from the religious community. The church in many societies is demonstrating that it is the most significant reservoir of human resources. Group number two represents those who are moving from the "formal" church to the "informal" church (from a view of the church centered on the body of Christ to a view of the church centered on the people of God dispersed in the world). The task of the clergy in regard to this group is to equip and encourage them to move out rather than holding them back in some kind of protective custody. For this group the boundaries of legitimate Christian action are being enlarged to what might be called the "public parish."

Critical Activists

Group number three represents those who have been engaged in direct political action and perhaps for a time even alienated or disconnected from the "formal" church (not "drop-outs" but "drop-aheads") but who through their experiences have now become aware of a need for fundamental change in the values and beliefs of society. They might be called critical activists. They are apt to be very critical of the institutions, including the church; yet they have become aware that the depth of resistance and fear touches religious roots. Therefore, they are seeking to get at the deeper questions of value and belief which lie behind the social systems. In this group are many people who are very open to contact with the religious community because they have become aware of its potential as a force for change in values and beliefs.

Often people in this group are more aware of the potential of the church than the church itself. An interesting affirmation of the religious function of the church is coming from this third group as, for example, indicated in the famous Kerner Report which called for fundamental change in the heart, mind, and spirit of the white community in America in order to overcome its deeply embedded racism. The temptation of group three, however, is to give up too quickly on the formal church. Ways need to be found to bring this group into contact with those within the formal church to link their efforts with those within the religious community.

Hopeful Evangelicals

The fourth group represents those who have crossed over back into the life on the religious community out of frustration, despair, or a deep awareness of the need for spiritual rootedness. These are the people who have found themselves driven back to the fundamentals as a result of their exodus experience into the world. Among these are many who are attempting to change the church by restoring its primary function as a movement of love and justice which might leaven the human community. They are seeking to conscience-tize the church. They are the "returnees" who may not fit easily into the life of the religious community and may ask embarrassing questions but who have the potential of helping the church reroot itself in its own spiritual soil. So we might call them the hopeful evangelicals. In this group, of course, are some who may be simply seeking escape from the ambiguities and frustrations of a life of social engagement. That is the particular temptation of this group.

Each group represents a valuable and essential emphasis in the life of the church, but each is different. Each is approaching or has passed through a cross-over point of exit or entry, a point of change in direction. The diagram below illustrates the position of each group and the potential movement that it represents. The concern here is to illustrate the need for symmetry in the complete development of the church. The diagram also illustrates how different groups may eventually move to another point themselves and thereby gain an understanding of where other people are. In fact we may even change direction.

Around both poles in the above diagram two forces are at work—a centripetal one and a centrifugal one. The first holds us to the one center, the second hurls us toward the other center. The gospel has both forces. On the one hand it draws us into a close-knit community of faith. On the other hand it pushes us outward toward the needs of our neighbor. Efforts to explain this push and pull, such as Luther's two kingdom theory, can easily lead to a kind of schizophrenia of religious and secular. Both centers belong to God and are proper places for the mission of God's people. We may change direction, as the diagram shows, but still there can be continuity to our mission. In fact one could argue that the centripetal and the centrifugal are really the reverse images of each other, like Alice in Wonderland going through the mirror. They become each other in the course of time and experience.

Translated into the language of faith, this means that evangelism becomes social action and that social action becomes evangelism. Both of these terms express aspects of the church's mission. They are not conflicting elements. Political action ultimately involves religious conversion. At the same time, concern for religious conversion is ultimately involved in political acts. Here we can learn much from African Christians who speak of the "whole gospel for the whole person for the whole society." The whole is not an aggregate of static points along the line, but a movement through time and place which affirms the great diversity in ways of expressing mission. The Christian life is often a confusing one, but it is also a very dynamic affair of withdrawal and return, gathering and scattering, religious and political activity.

5

Bread
for a Hungry World

Beatitudes for Global Consciousness

And seeing the multitudes, he went up into a mountain, and when he had sat down, his followers came to him to learn.

And he began to speak, and taught them, saying:

Blessed are those who are so oppressed they cannot hope for any release from exploitation, for theirs is the kingdom of heaven.

Blessed are those who mourn for loved ones who died nameless to the world because of exploitation, for they shall be comforted.

Blessed are those who are quietly steadfast in well-doing, seeking redress of others' grievances, for they shall inherit the earth.

Blessed are those who hunger and thirst after justice and right dealing with all persons everywhere, for they shall be filled.

Blessed are those who correct their own unmerciful practices, for they shall obtain mercy.

Blessed are those who seek the well-being of others with as much vigor as they seek their own benefit, for they shall see God.

Blessed are those who make peace between oppressor and oppressed that brings mutual liberation, for they shall be called the children of God. Blessed are those who are beaten, jailed, ostracized and otherwise persecuted for protesting distant or nearby oppression, for theirs is the kingdom of heaven.

Blessed are you when people shall revile you and persecute you and shall say all manner of evil against you falsely because you defended the oppressed in my name.

Rejoice and be exceedingly glad, for great is your reward in heaven, for so persecuted they the prophets which were before you.

Adapted from Matthew 5
by LaVonne Althouse

The Second Settlement of Earth

The sharing of bread is an urgent, do-able peace building task to share food and resources with the world's impoverished. It is one in which every person can participate directly. It is, therefore, "revolutionary" because it offers do-able, people-scaled opportunities which could rapidly multiply in epidemic proportions. The hunger issue, therefore, provides an immediate test case for the churches to mobilize their human resources for peace building. World hunger confronts those who have with the challenge to make basic changes in their values and lifestyle in order to avoid increasing conflict with those who do not have over the limited supplies in the world's pantry. Survival based on caring and sharing rather than conflict and exploitation is a necessary prerequisite for the "second settlement of earth."

The first settlement of earth had to do with the occupation of land and the control of natural resources. The first settlement of earth has been characterized by confiscation, exploitation, greed, and war. But now there are no new land masses to occupy. A geometrically expanding population faces the boundaries of limited resources. The cold fact is that the global community can survive only if it shares what is in the world's pantry. This basic economic or "bread" question lies at the heart of the changes facing us in the "second settlement of earth."

The prospect of not enough resources for a hungry world is a question Christ's disciples have faced before. In Luke's description of the feeding of the 5000 near Bethsaida we read, "Now the day began to wear away; and the twelve came and said to him [Jesus], 'Send the crowd away, to go into the village round about, to lodge and get provisions; for we are here in a lonely place.' But he said to them, 'You give them something to eat.' They said, 'We have no more than five loaves and two fish!'" (Luke 9:12-13). If we examine how Christ handled the "bread question" we may discover how we may undertake our peace-building tasks in the second settlement of earth.

The Bread Question

There was no escape for the 5000 people at Bethsaida from the fact of their daily needs. After the final chords of the Hallelujah Chorus had faded away, the last "Amen" uttered, and the benediction spoken, there, still unchanged, was the real world, a hungry world, before them. Perhaps in the crowd that day you might have heard someone say, "Religion may be a fine and uplifting exercise, and theological discourse may be inspiring and helpful for a while, but eventually you have to deal with the bread question. In the final analysis that's what life is all about. When the fine talk is over you have to get down to the basics of economics and politics. Let the religious leaders extol the spiritual truths all they want, it's the control of bread that makes the real difference."

Such questions have been raised many times since that famous event at Bethsaida. In 1848 there were riots throughout Europe as a result of the cruel effects of the Industrial Revolution, which crushed the lives of men, women, and even children in mines and factories. People cried for bread, for economic and political change. In that year a man who at the age of nineteen had once written an idealistic treatise on Christ observed the failure of Christians to respond to social injustice and took up an angry pen to write the *Communist Manifesto,* which described religion as an escape from the bread question. The author's name was Karl Marx.

Except for a few voices like that of Johann Wichern, who in the same year (1848) wrote the *Protestant Manifesto,* the churches did not deal with the bread question. Instead they denounced the uprisings and sided in with the powerful. In the pivotal year of 1848 the church had a profound opportunity to respond as Jesus did at Bethsaida and recognize that the bread question and the faith question belong together. An aggressive Christian action for bread and justice then would have removed much of the evidence the Marxists have used with great effect since to mount a persuasive case against Christianity.

Faith and Bread

Jesus' response to the bread question dealt with the two excuses most often raised by his followers. First, there is the question about getting involved. Is it appropriate for the church to get involved in such secular matters as bread? Second, do we have enough resources?

Jesus puts bread and faith together in his kingdom. Jesus fed the people that day as the natural thing to do. His disciples wanted to send the people away, to turn the problem over to others. The miracle was no trick to get their loyalty. Already at the outset of his ministry Christ had turned down that temptation— to turn stones into bread to gain a kingdom. Jesus fed the hungry because that is what love does—it responds, it serves, it gives.

Christianity does put bread and faith together. Here is no ascetic, sanctuary-confined religion, so heavenly minded that it is no earthly good, but a robust, earthly religion where bread and faith go together. Jesus did what comes naturally to those for whom God is lord of all of life. They feed the poor. Feeding the hungry belongs to the worship of God.

The People Question

Jesus' second response dealt with the excuse, "We don't have the resources." Here were five thousand or more hungry people. The disciples argued then and now, "Let the people forage for themselves, find inns and merchants, or let the government take care of that, or the welfare agencies. Why don't *they* not *us* do something about it." Jesus replied very simply, "Feed them yourself." Today we hear similar arguments even

99

though the hunger problem is far more complex. Hunger is a worldly problem and not the business of religion, according to many church people. They view bread as a material, political, and economic issue. They would transfer the responsibility to governments, multi-national corporations, and the United Nations. For them the world's hungry are not the problem of the disciples of Christ. But Jesus said, "Feed them yourself."

Is it an ironic twist of history and a monstrous contradiction, or is it a tremendous opportunity that the "have" countries today are those with the largest Christian churches and the "have nots" are nations with small minority churches? The loaves are in the hands of those who claim to be Christ's disciples. "Use what you have. Feed them yourself. You will discover that when you share what you have it will be enough." That was Jesus' response at Bethsaida.

The conviction that there is nothing that we can do thwarts at the outset even the modest acts of sharing what we do have. That apathy paralyzes the resources that do exist. Those modest acts take many forms including consuming less. In America that means less food for an obese nation and less natural resources consumed by an affluent society. Sharing involves land, water, air, fuel, and bread. Sharing what all of us have been given by our creator is the price for survival in the second settlement of earth. And this means not just land reform in Ethiopia, Chile and China but also in the U.S.A. where millions of acres continue to be stolen from the original inhabitants. The question is what you do with what you already have. "Feed them yourself." Sharing means going beyond acts of charity in today's world—to acts of social justice.

100

Despite the so called "aid" programs, the rich become richer and the poor poorer. In Namibia (Southwest Africa) the big corporations know that the years are numbered when they can continue to have free access to the rich natural resources there. Therefore they are accelerating their rape of the land, which will leave an already poor country poorer and some rich people richer—including many American stockholders.

Sharing must occur at many levels. It means a shift from private to corporate values. It means far reaching changes that will affect every one of us. And it will not get easier. World hunger is not a temporary condition, a brief setback on our continuing upward climb toward luxury. But what does this all have to do with the disciples and with us as ordinary church members? Most Christians cannot start with the big systems—governments and multi-national corporations—although many Christians are stockholders, or citizens with a vote, or literate people who can write to the congress and can speak up. All of us can start with what we have. We do have political power, consumer power, economic power. We do have at least five loaves. The accumulative effect of many small people beginning to share what they already have can make the difference.

The mystery of the kingdom about which Christ spoke is that it operates like leaven. The cumulative effect of the acts of lots of ordinary people simply using what they have is one of the best-kept secrets of this kingdom. One of the great unfinished tasks of the Reformation is the still largely unimplemented and revolutionary idea of the priesthood of believers, the church as people, God's people scattered all over the world, permeating every social structure. Each has a few loaves with which to do something. We rarely grasp the impact of that potential.

The Campus Corn Crib

"We could collect bummer lambs from the farmers, raise them and send the money overseas." The suggestion came from a member of a student group discussing what they could do for world hunger. "There is lots of corn left on the fields in our state after harvest," added another student. "I read a report recently that in this county alone between $1,000,000 to $2,000,000 worth of corn is left in the field."

This proposal caught the imagination of the group. Someone soon pointed out that the idea was as old as the Old Testament. A search of some Old Testament passages soon turned up Leviticus 23:22: "And when you reap the harvest of your land, you shall not reap your field to its very border, nor shall you gather the gleanings after your harvest; you shall leave them for the poor and for the stranger. I am the Lord your God." Soon a corn crib appeared on campus. Students and faculty alike joined in the effort to fill it from the field of cooperating farmers. The corn was to be sold and the money sent to CROP, an overseas church relief agency.

The idea spread and before long Gleaners International was born. The main purpose was not simply raising money, but the raising of global awareness among all who became involved. The story of the Gleaners spread through the mass media. One day a long distance telephone call from the director of the Heifer Project International confronted the Gleaners with an urgent request. In the neighboring state a group of farmers were staging a protest action and were about to slaughter some calves. The farmers were willing, however, to donate some of the calves to the Heifer Project if someone would go immediately to get them. A truck was loaded, and by driving through the night and through a blizzard the students were able to bring five calves back to the campus. A special corral was erected. After fattening, the calves were destined for Honduras where devastating floods had destroyed 500,000 cattle.

Through their experiences the students have learned that the problem of world hunger is a complex one. Technical, political, and distribution issues have to be dealt with. No simple solutions exist. But Gleaners International seeks to raise the moral questions. The corn crib and the corral on the campus of their college are visible evidence of this concern. And what may be more important, they helped launch a movement to glean a prosperous nation.

Tourists in a Hungry World

The crisis of world hunger has the potential of making the one-third of the earth's population which has conscious of the two-thirds which do not have. This exposure can be threatening. Contact can lead to conflict or to communication. Beyond the immediate sharing of bread there is the long range need for people-to-people sharing. This could take the form of superficial tourism, or it could mean the beginning of new local global communities. The following story illustrates how the contact between the two-thirds world of the have-nots and the one-third world of the haves begins right at home.

If the Shoes Fit...

Seated around the living room was a group of upper middle-class suburbanites assembled by an energetic local priest. They had been meeting for several weeks in a program called Communi-action. The group had played simulation games, watched special TV documentaries, read articles, performed field assignments and discussed. The purpose of the program was to make them aware of the problems of social injustice in their metropolitan area.

That night the issue to be discussed was welfare. "People should learn to stand on their own feet . . . . welfare recipients are lazy . . . . If the poor were willing to work they wouldn't be on welfare." Such comments reflected the feelings of many in the group as they began the evening session. Like many suburban tax payers they had little sympathy for and even less personal contact with the large numbers of poor trapped in the inner city.

A speaker-phone device had been installed in the home so that the group could interview resource persons over the phone. The voice of the person being interviewed was amplified over a loud speaker. That night this particular group telephoned a widow with four children who had agreed to share her experiences over the phone. The widow was on ADC (Aid to Dependent Children) funds which fact prompted a series of rather tactless questions from the group of how the widow was spending public funds. Finally one of the women in the group said to the widow, "Lady, if I were in your shoes tonight I would have more pride. I would go out and get a job so that my children could be proud of me."

Over the phone came the voice of the widow. The tone was quiet and even gracious. "Madam," replied the ADC mother, "you can thank God that you are not in my shoes tonight, for if you were you would be dying of cancer."

The awful truth spoken simply and quietly by the widow struck the group dumb. Their preconceived judgments and moral arrogance were exposed for what they were. No one could speak in the embarrassing moment of truth. Finally the leader hung up the receiver and turned to the group with tears in his eyes and said, "Is this the way we are treating people?"

In that suburb today are low-cost housing projects which have been initiated by members of that group. They had stood for just a moment in the shoes of an oppressed person and would not look at the world with the same eyes again.

Travel in Depth

The issue of world hunger could create new partnerships between communities in many parts of the world. Or it could create a lot of temporary tourists—people looking at the obvious but not seeing the root causes for poverty and hunger. A great deal depends on how we encounter each other and how deeply we look into our own communities. The problem with most tourism today is that people travel too quickly through each other's world. My own experience with travel leads me to believe that we perceive as deeply what is going on in another country as we understand what is happening in our own. In fact I wonder if a lot of travel isn't flight from our own local problems as well as from the problems of others. With pre-arranged bus transfers and Hilton Hotels at every stop it is no wonder that many American tourists visit but rarely "meet" other peoples.

Perhaps there ought to be a moratorium on tourism. Perhaps we need a time to understand our own local worlds before we can have meaningful world travel.

A tourist by definition is one who is not "at home" in a particular place but just "passing through." I believe, however, that touring groups can combine careful and sensitive reflection with travel and become effective learning laboratories for peace building. Since so many people are traveling today this could become a significant way to build global community.

A friend describes education as the gradually widening journey of the self into the past and the future and into inner and outer space. This idea is illustrated in a film which consists of a sequence of pictures taken of a person lying on a beach from ten feet, one hundred feet, one thousand feet up to 10^{10} feet. From that distance away all you see is the Milky Way. Then the camera explores the microscopic world of the person on the beach. The final scene from a distance inward of 10^{-10} reveals the atomic structure of matter and looks like the Milky Way. Perhaps that is what education is like. The deeper we explore the outer worlds the deeper we see into the inner world.

If we apply this concept to tourism, it would seem important to balance travel into outer geographic and social space with the exploration of inner space. The idea of Henry James that travel broadens the mind apparently doesn't hold true for modern travel which seems to separate the outer and inner worlds. Jet travel delivers one's body to another continent in a few hours, but the spirit doesn't arrive until two weeks later! By then the body is off on another leg of the planned tour and the two parts never do catch up.

If tourism is to be an effective way of building global community, some new ways need to be developed to help the body and spirit make the journey together. This would involve, among other things, the exposure of one's inner beliefs to the new and often challeng-

106

ing perceptions of other cultures. This requires a level of openness and trust, intimacy and honesty that takes time and careful preparation. That this has not been the case in most tourism is only too apparent, but that should not veil the tremendous potential of journeys made by the body and spirit together.

This generation in its lifetime will have traveled more miles than the total amount of all previous generations combined. But mere physical transport through space does not necessarily increase understanding. The billions of miles traveled by commuting suburban whites through black ghettos in urban America for decades and the continued insensitivities of these tourists to the world they pass through each day should remove any romanticism of the effectiveness of travel itself for raising consciousness.

Ties That Bind

From Canada have come two examples of tourism that show good promise of building understanding and long term partnership. One is called Tourism With Insight (TWIN). The program originated with church groups in Hamilton, Toronto, and Ottawa who approached tourism as an educational experience especially in the area of world development. They argue that tourism is an excellent tool for global consciousness raising, since everybody is apt to be a tourist some day. Their program involves excursions to the Caribbean planned closely with the Christian Action for Development in the Eastern Caribbean. Careful attention is given to the preparation of the tourist to make him or her aware of the economic, cultural, political, social, and religious effects of their travel. A style of tourism is being developed by TWIN which aids in the development of self-respect and self-reliance of the host country and in the humanization of the tourist as well.

The second program is Town Twinning. The idea of building personal and institutional links between towns in different countries began in France after World War II. Hundreds of German and French towns and cities are identified as twins. The effort in Canada has stressed the establishment of ties with communities in poorer countries. The exchange of teachers, city officials, business leaders, and above all ordinary citizens has the potential of global bonds that would be an excellent preventive medicine to war. What might have happened if 200 communities in Vietnam had been twinned with an equal number throughout the U.S.A. twenty years ago? The intimacy of ordinary people that would have been developed by such direct partnerships would have profoundly affected the economic, military, and political decisions between the two countries and might have prevented the tragedy of the past decades.

Another version of Town Twinning is being attempted between communities in the Upper Midwest and Mexico. A five-year program to develop global partnerships through local churches is being built on an earlier program which has involved hundreds of youth and their adult counsellors in something called "Mexican Youth Encounter." The twinning of the communities from which these people have come with villages and towns in Mexico is called "Covenant Communities." While such programs are only beginning, they do suggest that peace building is taking root at the local level and becoming a people's movement. The possibilities are there. The place to begin is right where you are in your local community.

6

Whole Earth Confession Checklist

Christians in medieval Europe used checklists for review of one's life prior to confession and Holy Communion. Often based on the Ten Commandments, they traditionally dealt more with personal responsibilities than with community or societal concerns.

For the 20th-century global Christian, a checklist for confession would deal appropriately also with sins of commission and omission involving our stewardship as members of the world community. Such a checklist could be developed for individual behavior, or that of one congregation or one nation.

We suggest here some sample questions and categories for a "Whole Earth Confession Checklist." We encourage you to develop your own particular guide, for use in personal, family, or parish settings.

A CHECKLIST FOR PUBLIC OR PRIVATE CONFESSION

A. God created the earth and saw that it was good, but we are rapidly destroying this creation and using up its limited resources. Examining this area of my life, do I

- use public transportation whenever possible to run errands, shop, attend meetings, theater, restaurants?

- restrict my use of air conditioning, power tools, household electric appliances to a minimum?

- when using my own automobile, do I organize my errands to hold trips to a minimum?

B. The resources of this earth belong to the whole of humanity, but about two-thirds of the world family is inadequately fed while one-third gets more than enough. Examining this area of my life, do I

- regularly review my patterns of consumption, starting with food?

- question the heavy use of fertilizers for my lawn and golf courses in my community?

- reflect on the use of foodstuffs to sustain the rapidly growing pet population in our culture?

- communicate with my representatives in national government about ways of stimulating production of more U.S. food surplus and getting it to those in need?

C. Our Western society has developed a money structure built on corporate investment. Where I invest, my funds are handled impersonally by boards I probably have never met, for financial endeavors with which I am not acquainted. Such endeavors often affect powerfully the lives of others, in my own society and other parts of the globe. Examining this area of my life, do I

- search out the uses made of my money in places I have made investments?

- look at the employment policies of firms my money supports?

- learn about the relationships the firms in which I invest have in overseas countries where dictator ships and racism thrive, perhaps with economic support from outside?

- question constantly whether the profits made by corporations in which I invest (and by myself) come at the expense of social justice in our society?

- know whether my investments support the making of war?

D. Western society seeks to operate through democratically structured political life. Examining my participation as a citizen in this process, do I

- concern myself with finding out the merits for the total society of the parties vying for my support?

- seek safeguards for minorities who cannot get support for their needs from the majorities which govern?

- become involved in a political party to influence its action for justice?

- encourage a free and full discussion of critical issues in our time with an honest look at all the answers suggested?

111

A LITURGY FOR THE CHRISTIAN PREPARING
FOR HOLY COMMUNION

Prayer Response to A: Lord, we come before the mystery of the bread and wine where the spirituality of your Presence becomes known to us strangely in material forms fashioned from nature. Through Holy Communion, release us to perceive your presence in all creation so that material things may reflect your holiness. Kindle in us ecological reverence for the spiritual fact of your material world. Amen.

Prayer Response to B: Lord, open our eyes so that we may see how everyone coming to your table participates equally in the unconditional sharing of your bread. Let this image of future, Kingdom economics come into the present time so that all may receive enough bread for their daily lives. Amen.

Prayer Response to C: Lord, the corporation sometimes makes mockery of your corporate flesh, given to us in the mystery of bread and wine. Let your people, joined in your corporate body at Communion, shape all other corporations in society. Educate us and give us discernment so that we may find ways of witnessing to your presence for the profit-making corporations in which we participate. Amen.

Prayer Response to D: Lord, we all come vulnerable to the table. Often we have hurt and have been hurt by the politics of living. Give us an ecumenical vision at the Supper so that we perceive your forgiveness for all our family gathered and for ourselves because of the fact of your remission of sin . . . for us and for many. Amen.

This material was prepared by Ewald Bash and Charles P. Lutz.

Models for Local Action

Data for this section gathered by Charles P. Lutz

These models for building world justice and peace are marked by several criteria:

1. They have *global pertinence,* that is, involve relationships among peoples of differing cultures, classes, or nations.

2. They are *replicable,* that is, the essential idea can be redone by others having comparable motivation and resources.

3. They include a *specific action,* as contrasted to a general program of education or sensitization.

4. They can be organized by *volunteers;* compensated staff not required.

5. They lead to *direct people interaction.*

1.

GOAL

Enabling international tourists to use the experience for *contribution* to human development, not *exploitation* of host peoples.

DESCRIPTION

Program seeks to prepare would-be tourists from North America for investment of their funds and their behavior in ways that will support liberation of Third World peoples and resist the domination assumptions implicit in standard tourist practices. Strong element of relearning, values-change, and support after return home built into program. Developed by Christians in Hamilton and Toronto, Ontario, with particular concern for Canadian tourists traveling to the Caribbean and other developing countries. A useful kit has been prepared. Workshops and seminars are arranged, including tourists, representatives of host countries, tourist bureaus, and travel agents.

MORE INFORMATION:

> TOURISM WITH INSIGHT (TWIN)
> 11 Madison Avenue East
> Toronto, Ontario M5R 252
> Canada   phone 416/924-9351

2.

GOAL

Showing how persons in single community may research and communicate the direct global connections that community enjoys.

DESCRIPTION

Model developed to illustrate global interdependence reflected by life in any city. Provides analysis of international impact the people in Columbus, Ohio, make —and the impact brought to them by the rest of the world. Looks at economic, educational, agricultural, manufacturing, and other systems. Data on Columbus and on many other U.S. cities is computer stored and retrievable for use in other communities.

MORE INFORMATION:

COLUMBUS IN THE WORLD/THE WORLD IN
   COLUMBUS
199 West Tenth Avenue
Columbus, OH 43201
USA

3.

GOAL

Encouraging affluent persons to form communities committed to simple style (modest consumption) and to global political action.

DESCRIPTION

What is called a Simple Living Movement is growing in North America. It is far more than young college dropouts. It runs the religious gamut from secular humanism to fundamentalist Christianity to radical Judaism. It is marked by a central conviction that middle and upper income North Americans can and should begin to let their own lives reflect a Just World Standard of Living. Much of the movement is also committed to active political participation toward building a more just global society. A representative group, which can provide information on similar groups as well, is listed below.

115

MORE INFORMATION:
    SIMPLE LIVING NETWORK
    4719 Cedar Avenue
    Philadelphia, PA 19143
    USA

4.

GOAL
Directing citizen pressure toward governmental decisions affecting world hunger and poverty

DESCRIPTION
Research on background facts and timing of upcoming actions in U.S. Congress and administrative agencies, informed by Christian theological understandings, is shared regularly with membership via well-documented newsletter. Individuals join ($10 per year), receive newsletter, may form local groups for activity as they choose. Central thrust: lobbying with representatives in Congress and with agencies of Executive Branch. Organization is directed nationally by ecumenical board. No direct appeal for funds or material aid, but such response through established agencies (e.g., Lutheran World Relief) is encouraged.

MORE INFORMATION:
    BREAD FOR THE WORLD
    235 East 49th Street
    New York, NY 10017
    USA   phone 212/751-3925

5.

GOAL
Providing on-scene sensitizing of local community

through full-time presence of Third World person(s) brought for that purpose

DESCRIPTION
Plan developed by local church in Hamilton, Ontario, brought Christian couple (wife and husband) from India for 10-day period of education and conscious-ness-raising in parish. Visiting resource persons were offered to many community groups and reached out through press also. Both Third World development issues and questions involving life/faith of church were treated. Couple came from Ecumenical Centre in Bangalore, are members of Mar Thoma Church. Second year: resource person from Trinidad.

MORE INFORMATION:
> OPERATION FIRE
> First United Church
> 400 King Street East
> Hamilton, Ontario
> Canada

6.

GOAL
Hosting and interacting with group of visitors from another part of the world

DESCRIPTION
Group of about 200 Christians from Japan, mostly laity and Lutherans, visited Iowa during September 1974. Stay of one week was hosted by Iowa District, the American Lutheran Church. Travel by charter plane was financed by the Japanese. Program of interaction planned jointly by hosts and visitors.

MORE INFORMATION:

> BRIDGE OF FELLOWSHIP
> Iowa District of the ALC
> 3125 Cottage Grove Avenue
> Des Moines, IA 50311
> USA   phone 515/274-3674

7.

GOAL

Training teams from North American communities for conscientizing work back home after living with organizing movements in Caribbean

DESCRIPTION

An intensive experience of Third World exposure for teams (5-6 persons) from USA or Canada communities who will work in their domestic struggles for justice and human liberation. Each team participates in two-month training process of action/reflection under leadership of a local organization in Greater Caribbean area (including Central America and northern South America). Aims to place liberation struggles of Third World peoples in North America into international context.

MORE INFORMATION:

> INTERAMERICAN TRAINING PROGRAM
> 1500 Farragut N.W.
> Washington, DC 20011
> USA

8

GOAL

Building movement of persons committed to non-violent conflict resolution at all levels, personal to global

DESCRIPTION

An attempt to link in an order, with specific disciplines voluntarily assumed, persons committed to a politically active, violence-renouncing style of life. Most participants identify with Lutheran theological tradition. "St. Martin" in the order's name is a simultaneous reference to Martin of Tours, Martin of Wittenberg, and Martin Luther King Jr. Loose national network tied together through a newsletter and sense of individual's commitments to discipline. Groups locally become support communities and renewal bases. No dues, but contribution for newsletter costs is welcomed.

MORE INFORMATION:

ORDER OF ST. MARTIN
c/o Larry Rasmussen
1701 Kenyon St. N.W.
Washington, DC
USA

9.

GOAL

Pairing of towns across national, cultural, and language barriers for mutual exchanges of all sorts, to people-to-people level, toward international peace, cooperation, understanding.

DESCRIPTION

An ambitious program, designed to give reality to common global citizenship which transcends political/national boundaries. Works for exchange in areas of culture, education, technology, economy, volunteer services, information, athletics, and language. Flow of exchange is two-way Twinning arranged through affiliation with international organization which maintains strict membership and performance criteria. United Towns Organization is a non-governmental organization in consultative and associative status with the UN Economic and Social Council.

MORE INFORMATION:

UNITED TOWNS ORGANIZATION
13, rue Racine
Paris 6
France

10.

GOAL

Mobilizing public pressure worldwide for release of prisoners of conscience and for the abolition of torture.

DESCRIPTION

Seeks to enlist concern and action of citizens throughout the world for release of prisoners of conscience and against the growing practice of government-sanctioned torture. Assists local groups to organize, provides well-documented research data and strategy assistance for action by citizens. Each local group

"adopts" three particular political prisoners somewhere in the world and works on their specific cases
in all feasible ways.

MORE INFORMATION:
> AMNESTY INTERNATIONAL
> Room 64
> 200 W. 72 Street
> New York, NY 10023
> USA

11.

GOAL

Organizing a townwide focus on justice and peace
concerns

DESCRIPTION

This locally organized Peace Week is put together by
a coalition of groups. Emphasis is on (1) international/
crosscultural issues close to home, e.g., situation of
non-German migrant workers in Germany; (2) horizontal rather than vertical learning—exchange of experiences among participants rather than presentations
by experts.

MORE INFORMATION:
> ACTION COMMUNITY PEACE WEEK
> c/o Falk Bloech
> Hahler Strasse 47
> 495 Minden, Germany

12

GOAL

Creating local ecumenical groups for development education by organizing intensive, week-long nation-wide focus on global development.

DESCRIPTION

National campaign in all Swedish churches is an annual event. During one week, meetings, debates, worship on international justice are conducted by congregations and local groups. Campaign is followed by studies and action groups on specific issues. Descriptions of the approach are available in English. Basic concept can be adapted into a local version anywhere in North America. Both sensitization and direct action by citizens are goals.

MORE INFORMATION:

ECUMENICAL DEVELOPMENT WEEK
c/o Svenska Kyrkans Centralåd Fack
104 32 Stockholm 19, Sweden

13.

GOAL

Identifying and linking up local resources for local parish and community action through People's Fairs, Parish Resource Fairs, Regional Resource Centers, mobile units and planning workshops of "resourcing." These programs are especially suited for small communities.

DR. ED SCHLACHTENHAUFEN
R.R. II
York
Nebraska, 68467 USA
Tel. (402) 362-3063

REV. WARREN SALVESON
Lutheran Resource Center
Clear Lake
Iowa, USA
(515) 357-4451

14.

GOAL

Providing ordinary people with a catalogue of involvements for global justice and peace including doable things for holidays, birthdays, and other celebrations plus hundreds of practical ideas for local and home involvement. Among items available is the *Alternative Christmas Catalogue*.

MORE INFORMATION:

ALTERNATIVES
1500 Farragut St. N.W.
Washington, D.C. 20011 USA
Tel. (202) 723-8273

15.

GOAL

Developing direct partnerships between communities in the USA and Mexico known as Covenant Communities so that people to people involvement in each other's human development might forge long term interdependent relationships.

MORE INFORMATION:
COVENANT COMMUNITIES
P.O. Box 19096
Diamond Lake Station
Minneapolis, MN 55419 USA
(612) 825-5326

Educational Helps

Prepared by Charles P. Lutz

1. *Multinational Corporations and Church Investment.*
   Documentation on investment by major U.S. religious organizations in firms doing business in Third World settings. Data on both amount of church investment and evidence of social responsibility displayed by corporations.

   CORPORATE INVESTMENT CENTER
   475 Riverside Drive
   New York, NY 10027 USA

2. *Internationalizing of Mission.*
   Findings of a month-long consultation in late 1973 in which eight overseas Christians observed and critiqued the life and mission of U.S. Lutherans. The report of the consultation ("We Declare Our Interdependence"), a guide for discussion groups, and a film are available.

   LUTHERAN COUNCIL IN THE USA
   Communication and Interpretation
   315 Park Avenue South
   New York, NY 10010 USA

3. *Programme to Combat Racism.*

   Facts and interpretation concerning effort by international ecumenical organization to identify with movements for racial justice and liberation in many parts of the world. Grants of money have been made to a variety of groups, some of which employ violence in struggle against military oppressors. Ask for publication "A Small Beginning," $2.

   WORLD COUNCIL OF CHURCHES
   475 Riverside Drive
   New York, NY 10027 USA

4. *Global Education for Christians.*

   A seven-unit course prepared for use by Roman Catholic educators, but useful also in non-Catholic settings. Topics included: "Three Worlds," "American Dilemma," "The Right to Develop," "American Power," "Charity Justice." Ask for "Justice in the World Primer," 50 cents.

   UNITED STATES CATHOLIC CONFERENCE
   Division of Justice and Peace
   1312 Massachusetts Avenue NW
   Washington, DC 20005 USA

5. *Shalom Seminars.*

   Resources and suggested pattern for U.S. Lutheran women to gather at local levels for study of peace/justice questions during 1976. Planned by cooperating committee of ALC, LCA, LCMS women's organizations.

   LUTHERAN WOMEN'S COOPERATING
      COMMITTEE
   c/o Edythe Daehling
   2900 Queen Lane
   Philadelphia, PA 19129 USA

6. *Namibia Education and Action.*
Information on educational resources and action efforts concerning the struggle of Namibia, the southwest Africa area seeking independence from illegal control by South African government. Namibia is the country which is most clearly the legal and moral responsibility of the entire international community. It is of particular interest to the Lutheran international family because one-half of its population is Lutheran and church leaders have been outspoken in challenging the South African oppressors.
LUTHERAN COUNCIL IN THE USA
Office on World Community
315 Park Avenue South
New York, NY 10010 USA
Tel. (212) 677-3950

7. *Third World Study Materials for Christians.*
Great variety of popular publications on world hunger/poverty/development issues, with biblical-theological basis. Prepared by Roman Catholic missionary order. Write for free catalog.
ORBIS PUBLICATIONS
Maryknoll, NY 10545 USA

8. *Publications on Liberation of Western Hemisphere Native Peoples.*
Materials on situations of peoples called Indians in both North and South America. Introductory packet, $2. Ask for catalog.
AKWESASNE PUBLICATIONS
Mohawk Nation
via Rooseveltown, NY 13683 USA
Tel. (518) 358-4697

9. *Materials on Economic Exploitation of Third World.* Publications dealing with specific world market cases (e.g., coffee, bananas, sugar) in which the rich nations continue to maintain trade arrangements highly advantageous to them, widening the gap between poor countries and rich. Ask for catalog.

THIRD WORLD FIRST/HASLEMERE
Britwell Salome
Watlington, Oxford OX9 5 LH
England